CRASH COURSE ON CHRISTIAN ETHICS

Crash Course on Christian Ethics

Colin Brown

Hodder & Stoughton

LONDON SYDNEY AUCKLAND

Crash Course on Christian Ethics
Copyright © 1998 by Colin Brown

The right of Colin Brown to be identified as the Author of the Work
has been asserted by him in accordance with the Copyright, Designs and
Patents Act 1988.

10 9 8 7 6 5 4 3 2 1

British Library Cataloguing in Publication Data
A record for this book is available from the British Library

ISBN 0 340 72150 2

Typeset by Palimpsest Book Production Ltd, Polmont, Stirlingshire.
Printed and bound in Great Britain by
Mackays of Chatham PLC, Chatham, Kent

Hodder and Stoughton Ltd
A division of Hodder Headline PLC
338 Euston Road
London NW1 3BH

Acknowledgments

This book would not have been written without the help of so many people. First there are all those students who have so willingly discussed these matters with me over many years, and helped me clarify my thoughts. Then my warm thanks are due to Emma Sealey of Hodder & Stoughton, who has not only seen this book through to publication, but also offered shrewd comments on many occasions. To Barbara Steele-Perkins my thanks for patiently reading and commenting on earlier drafts. Finally, a big thank-you to my wife Shirley for her patience and support as this book was written.

Colin Brown

Contents

Introduction

We live in a world which is divided in its response to things like test-tube babies, the Lottery, homosexuality, abortion, divorce, and much else besides. The list changes from time to time. Our grandparents may have been concerned about things like temperance and gambling, and our grandchildren will probably have a different list again, but in our time we have our own particular issues that affect what we do and the kind of lives and society we have. In some cases the issues that concern us arise from what we or other people do, or want to do. At other times we want to have informed opinions about things we read in the newspapers, or hear on the radio or television. So it is no surprise that many of us feel the need for help in knowing what is the right thing to think and do, and books that help us in this are most welcome.

This is a different kind of book. It is of great importance to us to ask how far journalists ought to go to get a story, or whether it is acceptable for people to cohabit, or whether a woman should be allowed to use the frozen sperm of her dead husband in order to conceive, but specific answers to some of these questions are not what this book is about. It is about a far more fundamental question, namely, how we decide the rights and wrongs of the way we and other human beings behave. In particular, this is a book about how we might come to our decisions if we wish to adopt a specifically Christian point of view about the way we live and behave.

Not all the decisions we have to make are important for ethics. Whether I choose salad or a sandwich is not in itself of moral significance. There is nothing about that decision which carries any implication that I *ought* to choose one rather than the other. On the other hand, there are issues of birth, death, human relationships and our life together in a community, which seem to most of us to carry the possibility that we ought to do one thing rather than another. We may not always agree about what we think is appropriate behaviour, but at least we recognise that it is appropriate to think and talk about what we *ought* to do.

Perhaps we can see this distinction if we think about the way we treat children. It may be aesthetically important whether we dress them in green or pink or purple, or whether the style of clothes we give them is the latest, but there is little in the way of an *ought* about what we do. But there are other ways in which we treat children that most of us think are morally wrong. We recognise that we ought not to abuse them sexually. Similarly, we are horrified when we have to face the evil of children being shot or neglected. There may be morally grey areas in the way we treat children – for example, over the sort of discipline we impose – but it is not hard to recognise that some ways of treating them are morally insignificant and others are extremely morally significant. It is the ways in which we *decide* which human behaviour is morally right or wrong, and how Christians in particular might decide, that are our concerns in this book.

We face a changing world in which we find our cherished standards challenged, and we have to form new opinions or rethink what we thought were our firmly established principles. Ethics has a role in providing us with a way of facing these changes. Sometimes we have a gut feeling about the way we want to respond, an instinctive feel for this choice, rather than the alternatives. Having a way of responding that we think is correct is an enormous help to us. It provides us with the framework in which to think about the issues we face. Having such a framework can help us avoid the irrationality that often surrounds our decisions. We can be creatures of impulse and prejudice, but having a way of approaching moral decisions can help us focus on what is right and wrong. In other words, ethics can help us understand why we think as we do and help us change that way if we find it is unrealistic.

There are reasons for our moral decisions which we are not always able to put into words, but which are there, nevertheless. It is because there are reasons that there are so many books and articles about such things as new developments in medicine. Normally they argue for or against whatever the new development is, using different reasons to support their own case and reject that of their opponents. It is because we have reasons that from time to time committees of experts are brought together to examine a new issue in the light of what they consider to be relevant considerations. It is on the basis of what they take to be relevant reasons that they produce reports and make recommendations to help the rest of us form opinions about the moral problems involved. Ethics helps us to identify those reasons.

We usually talk of Christian ethics as though there is a single response to the moral dilemmas of life, but when we listen to what Christians say, and read their views, we soon find that while in some areas of life there may be a general consensus about what is an appropriate Christian position, there are other areas in which the differences between Christians are quite profound, despite claims that different groups reflect Christian values. As we go through this book we will see some of the reasons why this is so. Sometimes the reason has to do with different doctrinal stances, but often it comes from different ways in which Christians make their moral decisions and that is what we will explore.

Initially we will meet the officers of The League for Family Values who face a moral dilemma. We will look at the different ways in which they respond, and begin to appreciate the variety of ethical approaches to human behaviour.

As we go on to think about Christian ethics we find the same diversity, because Christians face the same dilemmas and use a similar variety of approaches. We will be thinking about some of the similarities between Christian and non-Christian approaches to ethics, and in Chapters 9–13 we will explore the major differences in their priorities and goals.

1

Dealing with a Dilemma

The warning in the Introduction that Christian ethics is not a monolithic set of ideas agreed by all Christians simply reflects something of the difficulties that we face when we try to identify a satisfactory way of deciding what is morally right. It is a complex matter and common usage offers us a number of alternative accounts. The dilemma faced by the officers of the fictitious organisation, The League of Family Values, will introduce something of this range of alternatives and illustrate how complicated ethics can be when we sit and think about it.

Sophie's Story

The highly respected secretary of the League is a lady called Sophie, who is married to John. One day, in the strictest confidence and to illustrate a point she was making, she confided in Mr Jones, who is the chairperson of the League, that her son was not fathered by John but by her brother-in-law, Barry. It transpired that at an earlier stage of their marriage the relationship between her and John was extremely difficult because Sophie was childless. They had both been tested at the local hospital, and the results showed that John was sterile. That was too much for him to accept and he vehemently insisted that he was fertile and that Sophie was the one who was infertile. The result was a growing tension between them that eventually grew so bad that there was serious talk of divorce, especially when John set a time limit in which he expected Sophie to become pregnant. It was very unfair of him, but it all made

Sophie desperate as she faced the prospect of her marriage ending, which was the last thing she wanted. She desperately wanted to save it.

Then she hit on what she thought was the solution. Out of desperation she asked Barry to give her a child, and in due time their acts of sexual intercourse resulted in her becoming pregnant, and her child was born. Sophie and Barry agreed that in the interest of the marriage, rather than admit that Barry was the natural father, they would let John think the child was his. John was overjoyed and felt quite justified in believing that the results of the hospital tests had been incorrect. The tension went from his relationship with Sophie and all talk of the marriage ending disappeared. In fact, as Sophie admitted, since the birth of her son her marriage was stronger than ever before, and they were a close, happy family

As chairperson of an organisation that stood for the sanctity of marriage, Mr Jones was shocked and struggled to know what to do when a leading officer of the League had such a story to tell. He became so distressed that after a while he felt he had to talk to someone, and asked three of his closest friends and colleagues in the League, people who were discreet and trustworthy, to meet him, and rightly or wrongly, he told them about Sophie's child. Asking them for advice as to how to proceed, he told them that he considered the motive of wanting to save the marriage was entirely right and proper, and was the sort of thing the League encouraged. Similarly, the result of Sophie's liaison with Barry was excellent. The marriage was not only saved, but was positively strengthened. Yet the fact that Sophie had committed adultery in order to save her marriage troubled him. He believed adultery was morally wrong, quite apart from destroying family life. Hence his concern. He was not a religious man, but he did have standards, and it was because he believed in the values the League stood for that he had joined it in the first place. He was aware that he had been told the story in confidence because Sophie thought he could be trusted, but this was so serious that he just had to get help. What ought to be done? Should Sophie be asked to leave the League? If she were to leave, then should they find a reason which would avoid John knowing the truth and the marriage being destroyed? Should he let the matter rest, yet continue as chairperson? Would his continuance amount to condoning the wrong he believed Sophie had done?

Was Sophie Wrong? Our interest in the story is not so much with the situation as with the approaches that people might take in dealing with it. Mr Jones's instinctive response is to look for moral rules which ought to be kept. If they are not kept, then an action is morally wrong. In ethical theory Mr Jones's approach is an example of what is known as a **deontological theory of moral obligation**. This is a theory that says that **actions are right if we fulfil our duty and wrong if we do not, and is seen as an alternative to the idea that actions are right or wrong because of their good or bad consequences**. In Mr Jones's case, he believes that Sophie's behaviour is morally unacceptable because of her intercourse with a man other than her husband. He believes it is the act which is intrinsically wrong. Like many deontologists, Mr Jones accepts that the good intentions of the adultery were achieved and the outcome was good, but he believes they have no place in the morality of what had happened. **Moral judgment must rest on the action itself**. Not all deontologists would agree with Mr Jones, though. Some believe that outcomes are a part of the judgment, but they never constitute sufficient grounds for saying an action is right or wrong. They are the sort of people who would say that Sophie had behaved in a morally unacceptable way, and 'besides, what if it had turned out badly and John had got to know that the child was fathered by another man'. For such people, the possible result is one of the things to be borne in mind, but at the end of the day the really important point is that adultery is wrong simply because it is wrong to commit such acts, and not because there may be unwelcome consequences. We will think further about deontologists later, because there is more to say about the kind of stance to ethics that Mr Jones takes.

Mrs Thompson, one of the people in whom Mr Jones confided, took a quite different view of the whole matter. She did not seem to think it was at all important, and thought that the whole incident should be forgotten. Mr Jones was surprised to hear such a view and tried to show her that for an organisation such as theirs to pretend it had not happened to one of their officers was a betrayal of their responsibilities. But she was not to be moved and eventually they began to have a heated argument. Eventually Mrs Thompson spelt out her reasons. She said that she enjoyed being a member of the League. It gave her great pleasure. She felt she was an important member of the committee and that made her feel good. The social activities were good too and she enjoyed them all. In fact, the League played a large part in her life and she did not want the pleasure she found there to be destroyed because Sophie had tried to save her marriage. The truth was out! If Mr Jones had done that course in ethics when he was a student he would have recognised that Mrs Thompson was reflecting a position called **ethical egoism**. Her position smacked of self-centredness and she wanted whatever was done to be in her own self-interest. When Mr Jones told her that she was being selfish and that big issues were involved in all this, she agreed. But she claimed that everyone seeks what is in their own interests and what makes them feel good, and at least she was honest about it and was not hiding anything of what she felt.

Mrs Thompson represents one of the positions we can take if we believe that the moral rightness of an action should be governed by the results that are produced. After all, morality is about maintaining or promoting what is good and right, and a case can be made which says that morality is all about maximising good. On this account an action is morally permissible if it maximises, or at least does not reduce the good, which comes from that action. The good consequences of the action are the things that give moral acceptability and determine whether or not the action is morally right or permissible.

The name we give to this kind of view of moral life is a **teleological theory of moral obligation**, by which we mean that **whether the action is right or wrong is determined by its good or bad consequences**. In so far as the saving of Sophie and John's marriage is thought to be a good thing, then those holding this view of ethics would be reluctant to challenge the morality of what Sophie and Barry did.

Not everyone who has a teleological view of moral obligation is like Mrs Thompson. Miss Argyle is another person Mr Jones talked to. She too was against Mr Jones resigning or Sophie being asked to leave. As far as she could see, on balance a lot of good had come out of the adulterous act and she felt there was no need for anyone to leave. As she said, 'If John got to know what had really happened and reacted badly, then we might need to think again. Obviously, if there is more hurt felt than good, then we have a problem.'

Miss Argyle is another who appeals to results in order to make her moral judgments, but when she thinks of the consequences of an action, they are not limited to her own interests. She has a more general view which looks for the maximising of the **general** good. Miss Argyle represents a lot of people who hold to a form of **'consequences' theory of moral obligation** that is much wider in its concerns than the view of Mrs Thompson.

Finally, Mr Jones talked to Terry, who is a young student who thought hard about family matters after his own unhappy childhood, and for whom Mr Jones had a great respect. Mr Jones thought that a younger person's point of view might be helpful. Terry wanted to get away from what he thought were the conventional ways of looking at these things and he was surprisingly blunt with Mr Jones. He said that he thought Mr Jones was too influenced by what others had told him in the past and by his fears of what might happen to the League. His advice was that Mr Jones should have the courage of his own convictions and be honest and true to his own beliefs. He advised Mr Jones to do what seemed right, irrespective of what others thought. Mr Jones had heard this type of thing before, and asked Terry what would happen to moral standards if everyone behaved in such an individualistic way. Terry's answer left Mr Jones yet more confused, for he talked about Sartre and Marcel and Camus, names only vaguely familiar to Mr Jones, and when he asked who these people were Terry explained that they were existentialists whose ideas caused a lot of discussion at the university.

The different people who became involved responded in different ways, all of which have their supporters. When we think about these responses it becomes clear that making moral decisions is not as straightforward as perhaps we thought. Before we think further about this situation in which Mr Jones and his friends find themselves it may be helpful to recap what each is saying. Figure 1.1 (opposite) lays out the different viewpoints.

How do we human beings make our decisions as to what is morally right and wrong? The answer is, in a number of ways. Most of us take a general line which reflects one of two main ways, both of which we have now met. One uses the consequences of our actions as the key to establishing what is right and wrong, and the other claims that actions are morally right or wrong quite apart from the results.

In this and the next chapter we will think further about these broad categories and without at this stage passing judgment on them, see some of the strengths and weaknesses of each, and also note that they reflect ways in which Christians may and do respond to moral dilemmas.

Using Rules

First, let us look at Mr Jones's position, with his belief that adultery is morally wrong. It is this belief, as opposed to those of Mrs Thompson and Miss Argyle, that is causing his problem of knowing how to respond as chairperson of the League. His position appears to be very clear and understandable. He does not want to be seen to be condoning behaviour that he considers to be both wrong and inappropriate for his organisation. In his view, condoning would make him a party to Sophie's and Barry's conduct.

We need to be clear just what Mr Jones's position is at this stage in the story. Some apparent deontologists, and this is

Figure 1.1

Mr Jones	Deontology	He believes that there is something intrinsically right about certain actions and something intrinsically wrong about others, and it is his duty to do what is right.
Mrs Thompson	Ethical egoism	She believes the consequences of the conduct determine whether it is right or wrong. It is right if it produces good consequences, but the good must be in her self-interest.
Miss Argyle	Teleology	Like Mrs Thompson she believes that the good resulting from an action makes the action good, but she believes the good has to be the general good.
Terry	Existentialist	He sees the need to make honest and open decisions, free from the conventions of society.

the ethical term for Mr Jones, would agree that adultery is morally wrong and that he should not compromise himself in this matter. But they may go on to argue that adultery is wrong because it destroys family life, or leads to unhappiness or is a bar to good relationships in general. In other words, if Mr Jones were to resign or ask Sophie to resign, it would be possible to give good reasons in terms of the effects of such action. But this would be giving a justification based on the consequences, and this is not his position at all. He believes that adultery is a particular sort of action that is wrong irrespective of the effects it might have. He is saying that adultery breaks a rule that expresses the moral acceptability or unacceptability of the action. He believes that there are features of actions themselves, quite apart from motives or consequences, that make them right or wrong, though just what those features are may be hard to identify.

Mr Jones is one of very many, perhaps the majority of people, who are concerned about moral issues. **They believe that there are certain specific moral rules which ought to be applied to life and obeyed**, not because society will collapse if we do not, or because we gain by doing so. In so far as we obey those rules we will do what is right, and if we disobey them we will do what is wrong. Mr Jones's rules say that we should not commit adultery because it is wrong, and similarly that fidelity should be observed in marriage because it is right. For him moral life is about following rules such as these.

Many Christians share Mr Jones's belief that there are a number of moral rules which ought to be obeyed. The Ten Commandments appear to be an obvious example of rules being laid down to guide our behaviour, and as such we ought to comply with them.

One of the main arguments in favour of this kind of ethical position is that it provides us with clear and specific statements about what is right and wrong. Moreover, such rules are usually taken to be moral absolutes. Whatever swings there may be in public opinion about certain kinds of behaviour, for example, about cohabitation, there are rules that always apply and ought to be obeyed. Perhaps it was because of a belief that society needed a set of rules that give an absolute 'bottom line' for moral life, that in 1997 it was reported that schools would be sent copies of the Ten Commandments. 'Honour your parents', 'Do not murder', Do not commit adultery', 'Do not steal', Do not lie', are often thought to be the absolutes of moral life.

There is a long religious tradition of a rule-based morality. In Deuteronomy, Moses is reported to have introduced a long series of commands about the way the Israelites were to behave when they entered the Promised Land. He said, 'These are the commands, decrees and laws the Lord your God directed me to teach you to observe in the land that you are crossing the Jordan to possess . . .' (Deuteronomy 6:1). At the end of the passage Moses and the elders repeated the charge to the people, 'Keep all these commands that I give you today' (Deuteronomy 27:1). The keeping of the rules, whether moral or religious, was clearly seen as the way to proceed. Joshua, in his turn, exhorted the Israelites to 'be careful to obey all that is written in the Book of the Law of Moses, without turning to the right or to the left' (Joshua 23:6). The same importance given to rules can be seen in Samuel's farewell speech, 'But if you do not obey the Lord, and if you rebel against his commands, his hand will be against you, as it was against your fathers' (1 Samuel 12:15). The Pharisees held this view of ethics and were scrupulous about Law-keeping. John Calvin, the reformer, claimed that God requires obedience to the divine Law and the Puritans took a similar stance.

Religious communities may well see moral life as expressions of divine will, but it is by no means only religious groups that appeal to a set of moral rules. Pro-life groups, for example, are made up of those of different or no religious persuasion, yet they have a common belief that there is a moral rule that makes abortion morally wrong. Some believe it is wrong in all cases and others that there are some cases, usually carefully delineated, in which abortion may be acceptable. For them the maxim is not 'abortion is morally wrong', but it will be something like 'abortion is morally wrong except where the mother's life is in danger if the pregnancy is continued.' Both are rules, though, and are expressions of a deontological approach to ethics.

Our fictitious Mr Jones found it difficult to cope with his moral position. His rule was clear that adultery is wrong, and he did not want to be thought to be condoning such behaviour. Yet at the same time he sought advice as to how to proceed with Sophie. Perhaps he felt something of the dilemma which such a rule-governed position can present. For example, there are times when we may sense that there ought to be room for an exception to the rule that we follow. A local council may have a rule that pets are not allowed in their blocks of flats, and we may think it is a reasonable restriction. But perhaps we learn that an elderly lady, living alone on the seventeenth floor, keeps a budgie. She is unable to get out and has no visitors apart from the home help who comes in twice a week. Let us suppose a local council official hears that she keeps a budgie and insists that rules are rules and no exceptions can be made because once one exception is made there will be a stream of other people wanting to be treated as special cases and keep pets. Once one exception is made there will be bad feeling in the flats as one person is allowed to have pets and another is not. We may understand his problem, but it seems absurd that this particular lady, with her limited amount of contact with other human beings, should be deprived of the company of her bird.

A more familiar problem is that of keeping a rule which says that we should tell the truth in all situations because telling lies is morally wrong. We may think it is an excellent rule to have, but many of us face situations where a lie appears to be more appropriate than telling the truth. To tell the truth to people who are fatally ill can sometimes be destructive at a time when they need reassurance and encouragement, and we may think that in such circumstances our rule seems harsh. At times telling lies, or at least being economical with the truth, has a very useful social function. It enables us to maintain relationships when the truth would cause rifts and anger. If we always told the truth when someone asked us if we liked their new clothes or the meals they cook for us or the presents they give us, we could soon find ourselves without friends!

It would be possible to make new rules to cover such situations. We could say that occupants of flats may not keep pets except when they live on the fifth floor or above and only meet another human being twice a week . . . Similarly, we could decree that we should always tell the truth except in cases where . . . We could continue to add our conditions, though we might have some difficulty in building in all the exceptions we want to make.

The problem of the exceptional case can be seen in our legal system, where laws have to be redrawn when they are found to be too stringent or too lax. Ideally rules need to be such that they include the cases we think should be included and exclude those we think should not be included, and that is true of moral rules as well as our legal code.

If we think again of the elderly lady living her lonely life in her flat, it would be helpful to ask precisely why the rule banning pets seems so harsh. An obvious answer is that her life would be greatly improved by having the company of her pet. Similarly, if we ask why a lie may, if appropriate, be told to someone with a serious illness, we might want to say that it would enable him to live the rest of his life free from fear and distress, and this is a good thing.

In both cases we are claiming that the consequences of our exceptions are such that it is valid for us to break our rules. In fact we are recognising that there is some strength in what we earlier called the teleological theory of moral obligation where good consequences or results of our actions justify our behaving as we do. It is often the sense that the results of what we do are important, that causes some people problems with living consistently with the kind of specific rules we have been considering.

There are other problems with this kind of rule-governed ethic. Suppose two rules conflict? I may have a rule that telling the truth is right, and another that says that killing people is wrong. It is possible to imagine that there may be a time when telling an assassin the truth could lead him to the person he intends to kill. Or maybe a man has a rule that everything should be done to support the institution of marriage, and another that children should be given a stable environment in which to grow up, and yet another that says that truth telling is right. How then is he to react when he has been unfaithful to his wife and has every reason to think that confession will destroy his marriage and damage his children? Here again there are rules that conflict. We can see the problems that can arise within an ethic that is based on a series of specific rules that we think ought to determine our conduct.

There is a further possible drawback in this way of doing ethics. A catalogue of moral rules appears to offer the hope of a consistent and universal framework to guide our behaviour. But for that to be so we would need to agree on a way of deciding what the rules are to be. Such matters are not as easy as they may at first appear.

Christians who have a rule-governed ethic have traditionally appealed to the Bible for their rules, but there is a serious question to be asked about the appropriateness for our present culture and times of rules laid down in another culture at another time. Those who look to the Bible for their rules would no doubt respond that the Bible is culture free; if only we understood it aright, they say, and recognised that it is God's Word to the whole of mankind, we would see it is applicable to all cultures at all times.

The problem is that we are part of our own culture and times and we read the Bible in that context. Simple observation suggests that we obviously do not always understand it. One generation understands its moral teaching in one way, while a subsequent generation sees it in a different way. In the middle years of this century we have seen some sections of the Church claiming that activities such as ballroom dancing, going to the theatre or cinema, the use of make-up by women, eating out on Sundays, or taking alcohol, are quite inappropriate for a Christian lifestyle. Yet, at the same time, beer drinking was accepted as a normal part of a meal among many Christians of the same theological persuasion in Europe. In the same way, while eating out on a Sunday was thought by some Christians in Britain to be wrong, their theological counterparts in America saw it as a normal thing to do.

Finally, in this catalogue of difficulties for those like Mr Jones, there is the danger that what can be a helpful, structured framework for moral life can lead to a legalistic approach where the rules are followed with such attention to detail that they diminish rather than enhance moral life. This was one of the aspects of the Jewish religious establishment that Jesus found so hard: 'Woe to you, teachers of the law and Pharisees, you hypocrites! You give a tenth of your spices – mint, dill and cummin. But you have neglected the more important matters of the law – justice, mercy and faithfulness' (Matthew 23:23). Of course, it may be that a legalistic approach, that can tolerate no weakening of the demands of a moral rule in any circumstances, is seen as a virtue by those who hold such a position. But for many people there is something harsh about being so bound and controlled by the rules that they must be obeyed at all costs. We must make up our own minds as to whether that is what moral life is about.

There are problems, then, with a specific rule-governed ethic such as we have been thinking about. On many issues it can provide clear statements about what is morally right and wrong. With some justification it can be claimed that without a set of moral rules we cannot know with any certainty how to behave in morally good ways. Yet there are obvious difficulties, though for many who live by such rules these are more theoretical than practical.

Basic Principles

There is another way of looking at deontological theory that may enable us to overcome some of the pitfalls. Rather than seeking to list specific rules that have application to particular forms of behaviour, this version of the theory is far less limiting. This alternative view sees the rules as being more general in character. One example would be the injunction to do to others as you would have them do to you. As a rule it lacks the precise application of the 'do not hurt other people' kind of rule, but its very imprecision is its strength as well as its weakness.

These general wide-ranging rules act as fundamental principles on which to base our moral lives, and as such give us the guidelines with which to approach new situations about which we have not previously had to make moral judgments. We still have to work at our decisions, but we do so within the framework of some broad principles of moral life.

For Mr Jones such a wide rule would enable him to view possible responses to Sophie's confession from a broader point of view. More considerations come into play than his immediate response. This need not mean that he has to compromise on what he sees as a serious moral lapse, but it puts it into a wider context. In so doing it enables him to live more comfortably with the variety of moral considerations he faces.

On the other hand, the imprecision of such a rule means that there are less likely to be ready answers to making moral decisions. We cannot read off one particular response when we seek to obey the rule to treat others as we would like to be treated. With such wide rules we really have to make decisions, the danger being that with hindsight we may find we have made the wrong one. What we took to be right at the time, on further reflection we believe to be wrong. To accept this form of rule-governed theory may rob us of a certainty we might have felt with the more specific form of the theory. Yet our psychological state is but one factor in deciding which of the wider or narrower versions we find most satisfactory.

Let us return to the story of Sophie's adultery for a moment. While Mr Jones was wondering what to do, he thought it right to tell Sophie how worried he was about the situation and that he was considering either asking for her resignation or resigning himself. When he spoke to her she was furious. She could see no reason at all why anyone should resign, as her intentions had been honourable and the outcome of her liaison with Barry was not just a marriage saved, but a closer relationship with her husband. If The League for Family Values really wanted to promote better marriages she could not understand why there was a problem.

In her instinctive response to Mr Jones, she accused him of being small-minded and not having any understanding or compassion for those seeking to save shaky marriages. Did he believe that marriages should be saved or not? she asked. We can see what she was doing. She was complaining that his ethic did not include some of the things she thought it should. She thought he was rejecting an ethic based on wide rules, and although he did not think in those terms, it did make him wonder if compassion ought to override his more specific beliefs about adultery.

Many Principles

Once Mr Jones got over Sophie's criticism of his rather narrow-based rule morality, he asked himself if there was a single moral principle that lay behind the rules that he had always accepted as showing him right from wrong. Soon he realised he actually held a number of principles, all general and all requiring him to work out how to apply them in specific situations. He could not be sure he could identify them all, but things like respecting the truth and other people's property came to mind. He realised that behind his belief that adultery is wrong was the principle that the sanctity of marriage should be maintained. Then he thought that something like 'all human beings should be protected from harm' ought to be added to his list. Of course he still felt very clear about some of the ways in which these general rules should be applied. Nothing was going to convince him that adultery was ever going to be anything but wrong, but he could see that he really did believe in some fairly broad principles which gave rise to the rules for his life.

Although he did not realise it (and why should he?) he was taking a point of view that was influential in the earlier part of the twentieth century, namely, that there are a number of wide rules which guide our morality, each of which guides us into particular ways of behaving. He did not go as far as some would and say that these principles do not impose absolute duties on us, but rather that they tell us the kind of things we ought to do when we face moral decisions, other things being equal. The principle ought to be followed if there is no other principle that supersedes it in a given situation.

For example, two such principles that have been suggested are that promises should be kept (other things being equal) and other persons should not be injured (other things being equal). We can imagine a situation where promise keeping would lead to a person being injured, as when keeping a promise to return a sharp tool to someone who has become mentally unstable and is threatening to kill a neighbour. We might want to say that promise keeping is a fine principle to have, but in this situation other things are definitely not equal. We have a conflict between principles, even though they are now much wider than the specific rules we thought about earlier.

If there are no other overarching principles, these conflicts have to be resolved by weighing up the pros and cons of the various principles and coming to a decision. It could, of course, be argued that the answer to that problem is to decide that some principles are more fundamental than others, but the number and status of any principles have to be true to facts. It means that, as in many ethical positions, there is no alternative than to ask the right questions of the situation and struggle to get what seems to be the right answer.

Mr Jones could see that a rule-governed theory which deals in principles rather than specific rules still leaves us with problems, but it may be that life is like that. Maybe it is a fact of moral life that there are no easy answers.

Finding a Single Principle

Not all ethicists accept that there are a number of basic principles, and there have been various attempts to advance a single principle that will give the moral direction we need. A simple way of using a single principle is to assume that **an action is morally right if it is legal**. The moral rule here is that we ought to obey the laws of the country and, in general, so we ought. Not many of us would want to use that as a basis for our moral decisions, though, because some of our legal rules may be morally wrong.

Sophie's case is a good illustration of this. She has a legal right to have a child by Barry, but that is not the same as saying that she has a moral right to do so. The moral question remains to be answered.

A much more sophisticated attempt to find a single principle was that made by Immanuel Kant, who was a German philosopher living in the eighteenth century. He claimed that **when we have to make our private moral decisions about an action, we need to ask if it is one that we can consistently will that it be applicable to everyone facing a similar situation**. The word used to describe this requirement is the cumbersome 'universalisability'. This expression simply means that **what is right for me in a given situation is right for everyone else in a similar situation**. If the answer is that our action is not right for everyone else, it is not universalisable and it is therefore wrong.

If we act on the principle that we should help other people only when we personally get something out of it, or when it is convenient to us, then Kant would say that we behave immorally. If we apply the principle of universalisability to such actions we would accept that others can only help us when it is convenient to them. But this is not a state that we would seriously want to apply because it could deprive us of help when we need it.

The effect of universalisability is that it protects the objective nature of morals. For acts to be committed in similar circumstances, there is no 'it is right for me but not for him'. To act morally is to deny exceptions in our own favour, but to recognise our place in humanity, subject to the same moral obligations.

The weakness is that universalisability is a procedural device, rather than one that settles issues of morality. For example, some may genuinely advocate cheating the Inland Revenue, and for political reasons will that everyone else does the same thing. Or a racist could claim that it is morally right to 'treat fairly only those of your own race'. They could hold that to be true for those other races as well as our own, but it leaves open the question of the moral standing of such a statement when we think of relationships between races.

Kant claimed to be expressing his principle in another way when he also stated the more familiar principle that **we should always treat human beings as ends rather than as means**. A good illustration of the link between the two statements is to be found in cases of rape. It is certainly not an act that we would want to make universal, for that would mean it would be morally acceptable for any of us to be raped. At the same time rape is a good example of behaviour which uses people as a means of personal gratification, rather than treating them as an end in themselves, with dignity and a will of their own.

Kant's principle of universalisability has some features that are attractive for traditional Christian ethics. It affirms the belief that there is something about ethical standards that applies to us all when we are in the same situations, and it denies practices which treat human beings as means rather than ends. In addition, it seems to be stating in a theoretical way what Jesus expressed in more concrete terms, 'So in everything, do to others what you would have them do to you' (Matthew 7:12).

Doing the Will of God

Whether Kant has stated a basis for Christian ethics that is theologically or practically adequate, is a further matter. A more obvious single fundamental moral principle is one which says, **only do what God approves, and always do it**. The adequacy of such a principle depends on the view we have of God. If we believe that he is so distant or different from us that he is unknowable to human beings, then we have problems in saying just what he does approve. On the other hand, if we believe that we have some way of knowing God's mind about ethical matters, then we can begin to put together lists of what is acceptable and unacceptable.

This principle seems to be a good foundation for a Christian ethic based on an idea of God who has in some way revealed his mind. The Bible is an obvious source of that revelation. But there are two difficulties we have to take into account before we accept this as the fundamental moral principle of Christian ethics: we have to face a practical limitation and a philosophical challenge.

The *practical limitation* is one that we noticed earlier and we can express it as a question. Is it possible to make a list of actions of which God approves or disapproves, when the revelation was given to a different culture at a different time from our own? If we can be sure there is a further revelation after the compilation of the Bible, we can perhaps keep our list of what is right up to date. We would need some way of being sure that we do actually know God's mind about some of the issues we face, for example, with the developments in medical science, which were unknown in biblical times. Unfortunately there are cases where people claiming to know God's mind have murdered others in response to what they thought they knew of God's will. Obviously it is difficult to be sure that we do know his mind about some of the moral dilemmas we face in the late twentieth century.

The *philosophical challenge* dates back to Plato, writing before Christ. Some philosophers argue that before we can use our knowledge of God's approval in order to judge what is right, we need a knowledge of what is right in order to decide that what God says is right, really is right. As Plato put it, is what is right because the gods approve it, or do they approve it because it is right? In other words, do we need to be able to recognise that God is telling the truth when he tells us what he approves? If so, then we need to know what is true in order to recognise it in God's words. Suppose a nurse claimed that a great revelation from God in a dream told her to kill all the patients in her care. We would say that we have a knowledge of right and wrong by which we can evaluate this supposed command from God. The purpose of raising these matters is not to seek answers at this stage, but to raise a possible fundamental moral principle which has obvious interest for Christian ethics.

So far we have been raising a number of alternative ways of doing ethics, all within the general ethical position known as deontology; in particular we have been looking at rule-governed positions. We have not yet looked at the option of using the results of our actions as a guide to our moral judgments. The picture is complicated and the alternatives many. We have looked at the option of using a series of specific rules, at more general rules that act as principles, at the option of using a number of such general rules and at the idea that there may be a single fundamental rule from which we can draw our ethical standards. Some of our alternatives have obvious links with some of the practices used by Christians and we could appeal to more than one of them and claim this is what Christians actually do, or even make the stronger claim that this is the basis of Christian ethics.

2

Living without Rules

So far we have been looking at the kind of approach that Mr Jones found helpful in dealing with the problem that Sophie's behaviour posed for him. We have thought about some of the different positions that people take even when they all advocate the use of rules of some kind. We now turn to some alternative views that do not look to rules, though they also reflect the view that moral right and wrong is to be decided by the action rather than the intentions or consequences. These alternatives have in common the belief that there is no class of action that is always right or wrong in itself. Rather, actions are always particular. It is always a specific action and the fact that it takes place in a particular situation that makes it different.

Looking at the Context of our Actions

Our actions do not take place in a vacuum or laboratory conditions. They have a context. As we will see in Chapter 3, there is an influential position that sees this fact as being of major importance in Christian ethics. For people who think in this way, the result is that the question we should ask is not, 'What is the right thing to do?' but **What is the right thing to do in this situation?'** This view of ethics means there are no specific rules that always apply in any situation. 'Always tell the truth' is not very helpful if we follow this way of viewing ethics. There is no list of obligations of this sort, from which we can simply select the appropriate rule, irrespective of the situation involved. It is the particular action that has to be examined and reacted to. If we allow that the context of our actions is significant in making our judgments, at the back of our minds should be the thought that '**in these circumstances I ought to tell the truth, but in a different situation when the question of truth telling arises, I ought to consider the matter anew**.' To see this approach in practice, we will confine ourselves to the two forms it can take.

Intuitionism. One theory that denies the need for rules in our decision-making but still accepts that the issue turns on the action, is known as **intuitionism**. The idea here is that **rules are unnecessary because we possess an immediate moral awareness**. A parallel has been drawn between an awareness of beauty and that of moral right and wrong. Just as we do not need rules to tell us what is beautiful so with what is morally right. We just know such things.

Renford Bambrough illustrated ethical intuitionism by telling a story in a BBC Radio 3 broadcast. He asked his hearers to imagine a small child rushed into hospital following an accident, where the doctors decided to operate. Bambrough claimed that if there is anaesthetic available, there is no need to ask if it is morally correct to administer it – we simply know that it should be used without having to ask for moral justification. He went on to say that if we were to say that no anaesthetic should be given, we have not understood the situation in some way, because if we understood, there is no doubt about the obligation to ease the pain

If we allowed this intuition to operate we would know intuitively when particular acts should be done or avoided. It is something like the 'gut' feeling we sometimes have about the rightness of situations in which we find ourselves.

Existentialist ethics. A second example of this emphasis on particular actions that focus on the act rather than on any rules, is that of existentialist ethics. This is difficult to describe because existentialist ethics is more a family of related ideas than one theory that can be conveniently defined. Some existentialists are Christians, others are atheists, but they are united in a common approach to moral life, rather than in a detailed moral code or method. **The basic premise is that individuals have to take responsibility for their own lives and in so doing have to devise their own morality and make their own choices**. Moreover, those choices have to be made with honesty. A good deal of our life is likely to be spent within the constraints of others' expectations and our own desire to conform to the conventions of our society. The result is that we tend to act parts and behave in ways that are not true to our own personhood. This is the point that Terry made to Mr Jones when he told him to be himself, rather than being influenced by the views of others.

Two ideas characterise existentialist ethics. First, **we are conscious beings with a freedom to make our own evaluations about each situation and to make choices**. With that goes a responsibility for our actions and for the guilt and shame that may follow them. How we see things and the ways in which we react to life, are for us to own – hence to be true to who we are we have to accept responsibility for the choices we make. Freedom, though, is not simply a personal quality to be grasped. It implies acknowledging the freedom of others and acting in ways that respect and preserve it.

It means recognising others as persons, not middle class or working class, dustmen or stockbrokers, lazy or busy, church members or pagans, or anything else. They are persons in their own right, just as we are. To respect their freedom is to see them as having their own plans and dreams and hopes, and giving them the space to pursue them.

Second is the idea of '**bad faith**'. We act in bad faith when we deny our freedom and say things like, 'I cannot help it', or we pretend to be what we are not. We withdraw from the reality of ourselves. We act the part of what we think others want us to be and allow them to take from us our freedom to be who we are. We allow them to determine the kind of person we are to be. We may feel comfortable when others tell us what to do. They may guide us into a way of life from which good comes, but when it stops us taking charge of our lives and taking the decisions that are true to us, then it is wrong. Acting in bad faith, then, takes us away from our moral integrity and leads us to do what others think is applicable either to us alone or to everyone else.

Instead of moral life being governed by rules, duties or principles, the existentialist invites us to look at each situation free from any such constraints. We need to put stock answers and other people's norms behind us. It may be that in looking at each situation, free from the constraints of convention and norms, we will come to the same conclusions as those who follow the norms of society. So be it. The important thing is to take our own decisions, rather than being driven by others.

Existentialist ethics, then, is about being authentic human beings rather than moral clones. The responsibility for moral life is ours and ours alone, and to fail to accept that is to be less than true to what it is to be human.

It is difficult to criticise existentialist ethics, in part because it takes so many different forms. It is more a general approach to moral life than about holding particular views. There is much more to be said about it, but my brief account will have illustrated a view of ethics that does not look at norms or rules for its content.

Once again, no doubt, there is much here that will attract Christians. The emphases on respecting freedom in oneself and others, and the need to live authentic lives, have all been advocated by Christians – both those known as 'Christian Existentialists' and others – not least because they can be argued for as arising from a Christian doctrine of creation. Once again, though, it does not follow that this best fits Christian belief and teaching.

We have been considering the responses of Mr Jones and Terry to Sophie's behaviour, and we have focused on a number of alternative ways in which we might give meaning to the claims that the morality of what she did is to be decided in the act itself rather than in the intentions or results. Some of the accounts we have thought about have obvious associations with Christian ethics. It is already clear that when Christians ask ethical questions about human behaviour, they may hold different views and may differ about the way they will make moral decisions. We still have to think about ethical positions based on the intentions and consequences of acts, and we will see that there are still more alternatives that Christians may wish to adopt. Before we continue we summarise in Figure 2.1

Figure 2.1

Looking for Right and Wrong in the Act

Rule-Governed Options

(1) **Specific rules** such as, Do not steal, Do not tell lies, Do not kill.

(2) **Principles**. These are wider rules which act as principles. Examples include respecting the sanctity of human life and respect for property. We may prefer to have a number of basic principles, or we may prefer a single basic principle. Examples we have thought about are

- obeying the law
- seeing if an action is what we want to be applicable to everyone
- obeying the will of God.

Options that do not Appeal to Rules

(1) **Intuitionism**
(2) **Existentialism**

the various options that we have met in looking at the action as the point at which to make a moral assessment.

Intentions

When Sophie was telling Barry about her talk with Mr Jones and her anger at what she saw as an overreaction on his part in talking of resignations, she said that if she had not intended to save her marriage, she would not have turned to Barry, and he understood that. Clearly her intention was a deciding factor when she considered whether she was doing the right thing in approaching him.

Sophie was correct in thinking her intentions mattered. We certainly take notice of them. Imagine that a girl tells us about a boy who is stealing apples. Our response is likely to be influenced in part by what we think is the girl's intention. If we believe she simply wants to get the boy into trouble we may tell her not to tell tales. But we may react differently if we believe that she is genuinely concerned for the boy's safety when climbing apple trees. In our society intentions to get revenge, or cause another person some harm, are simply not acceptable.

Intentions are notoriously difficult to pin down. We may say what we intend, but an observer may see that our intentions are not what we claim, or even believe them to be. We may think that when we tell others of our achievements, we simply intend to state facts and ensure that the truth is known. An observer may see that our real intention is to show how important and clever we are. What may appear to be a good intention to help an old lady by mending her garden gate, may really be that we want to be *seen* mending her gate. The preacher who says his intention is to glorify the Lord may really be intent on making a name for himself.

Fortunately we have some rough-and-ready guidelines that help us evaluate others' intentions. For example, we can look at a person's past behaviour, and notice the seriousness of that person's attempts to put the intentions into practice.

Sophie's appeal to intentions told us more about her own thoughts and values than about her actions. Intentions in themselves do not tell us anything about the morality of the act. A man who sees no future for his children because modern society is so evil and corrupt, may kill them. We may appreciate his intention to save them from such a society, and we may applaud his sensitivity and concern for his children, but there is still a question to be asked about the morality of murdering innocent children. If we ever stop to think of the morality of Robin Hood's behaviour, we find the same thing. The intention of helping the poor may be worthy. They tell us that Robin Hood was a kind and generous man. But we still have a question about the morality of stealing.

Our reactions to cases like these suggest that there is some other factor, or factors, involved that actually determines the morality of what we do. The very language of intentions gives us the clue that this other factor is usually an appeal to the outcome of the act. When we intend something to happen we are in fact looking forward to a new state of affairs that we think is desirable. We are looking for a result to our actions, and that is what we intend to bring about. Robin Hood intended to help the poor by robbing the rich. We intend to give an old lady peace of mind by giving her a gate that shuts properly. A man kills his child intending that she will be spared what he sees as the corruption of modern society. In each case talk of an intention is a way of saying what we wish the resulting state of affairs to be like. In so far as we approve of that result we applaud and encourage such intentions. Where the results are likely to be undesirable we deplore them.

Intentions in morality, then, lead us to approve or disapprove of the way a person goes about their moral life. It says something about the kind of person they are and what kind of a world they want their actions to promote. But it does not help us very much in deciding whether an action is morally right.

We need to move on to yet another aspect of our story,

namely, the way in which the consequences of the action had a place in the way people reacted to what had been done.

The End Results of our Actions

Miss Argyle had her own ideas about the morality of what had happened. You may recall that she agreed with Mrs Thompson that it was the result of what Sophie had done that really mattered. In contrast to her friend's insistence on measuring the results of behaviour in terms of her own interests, however, Miss Argyle had the wider view that we should look for the maximising of good in a much more general way. Holding such a view, Miss Argyle had a far more interesting and generally acceptable view of what is known as a teleological theory of moral obligation, *telos* meaning end or goal.

When we are bringing up children, we usually teach them rules for living: do not steal, always tell the truth, and so on. But we also say things like, 'What will happen if everyone did that?' It is not just with children that we combine both the actions and the consequences of human behaviour. In practice, society may be tolerant of those who do not pay their road tax, or bother to vote, or who fiddle their income tax returns. But when we want to give a reason why they are wrong, we sometimes ask what would happen if . . . We do not say what the consequence will be, but it is assumed to be against the general interest.

Usually a theory that looks to consequences decides what is right or wrong by the extent to which an action does or does not achieve what is good, however that is defined. For example, if we believe that good health is a good thing to achieve, then those things that promote it are good actions. It is right that we give food to the poor, support famine relief, develop efficient medical services, ensure there are welfare safety nets, encourage people to think about their diet, and so on. Wrong actions are those that would diminish the quality of our own and others' health. Actions such as taking harmful drugs, selling diluted milk, overwork and stress would be counted as bad, and it would be wrong to do such things. The 'good' of health has implications for the way we behave.

It is easy to see that some actions are instrumentally good. If health is 'good' then we would say it is right to provide medicine and eat sensibly. But why is health good? We could say that it is a precondition to enjoying life. So why is an enjoyable life so desirable? One answer is that it leads to a feeling of well-being, but again we can ask why that is good and worth having. We are in a chain of goals that it could be argued it is good to achieve, and they give us a host of activities that are right to do, given our ends or goals. But where do such chains lead us? We face the possibility that there may be one final goal which will justify all that is in the chain of things that are desirable. The chain will end when there is no further justification needed. The goal or end is intrinsically good, that is, it is desirable for its own sake, not for an instrumental reason.

Over the years people have suggested a number of possible 'goods' that may be intrinsic. One that has been popular in the second half of the twentieth century is that of **self-realisation** or the development to the full of our abilities and talents. Although it takes a number of forms, it is an attractive goal, reflecting as it does a concern for wholeness and individual worth which give both its content and goal.

Aristotle took the view that the intrinsic good is the **exercise of reason**. He argued that mankind shares a number of powers with other animals, but the ability to reason is unique to human beings. He concluded that this must be the true function of human beings, and hence rational activity is their intrinsic goal. It can be found in moral virtue and in intellectual value, the latter being the higher value because it is the unique supreme end for us.

You may find this an odd idea when activities like cooking and embroidery are also unique to human beings. It would be strange indeed to say they are of intrinsic value though. Nevertheless, those who have enjoyed the delights of grappling with intellectual problems sometimes find it to be an intensely satisfying activity. It is not only a psychological experience of worth, though. There is an inbuilt value in reason, for if we ask why anything is a good end, it presupposes that there are good reasons for the answer we give. The exercise of reason lies behind the questioning of instrumental goals, which suggests it is intrinsic to the very exercise of seeking an intrinsic end. That makes the exercise of reason a particularly unique activity on which our quest for good depends.

There have been other attempts to say what intrinsic goods are. One that attracts Christians is the claim of the Westminster Catechism. The answer to the question, 'What is the chief end of man?' is **'Man's chief end is to glorify God, and enjoy him for ever**.' This religious goal is like many of the others that have been raised at different times. It reflects personal values which will of course affect our views.

We do not have to identify just a single goal, though. It is quite respectable to have more than one intrinsic goal. For example, we might say that the pursuit of pleasure and of knowledge are both intrinsic goals, or there could be other combinations to make a case for.

The details are not our concern – we are looking at alternative ways of doing ethics, and can see the possible role of consequences in our decision making. Precisely which consequences are relevant for us is difficult to know, but they are certainly an important option for us in making our decisions.

The Greatest Good of the Greatest Number

Most people who seek right and wrong in terms of the consequences of what they do reject the way in which the Mrs Thompsons of this world equate what is right with what they can get out of it. Usually they seek to do what will produce the most good for everyone affected by what is done. They would say that to prefer my lesser good over other people's greater good is unjustifiable. These people say that we should produce as much good as possible. This theory is described as **utilitarian** and it has a long history.

While the theory does not require us to specify any particular good – and we have seen there are a number of goods we could invoke, both instrumental and intrinsic – the classical theory sees pleasure or happiness as the good to be maximised. Along with that is the further claim that pain and unhappiness are to be minimised.

This was actually the position taken by Miss Argyle. Her opinion was that if there were strict regulations over the behaviour of the society's officers, there would now be a general disruption among those who supported The League, and a lot of people would be hurt. In the interests of the general good, she thought it better if things were allowed to continue as though Sophie had never said anything at all to Mr Jones.

It may seem strange to make pleasure the good to be pursued, for it is notoriously slippery when we try to describe it. It is even more difficult to achieve deliberately, for what gives pleasure to one person may leave the next person depressed. We cannot be sure that what we do to give pleasure will be successful.

Yet, despite the practical difficulties of being precise in our definitions and practices, it has been argued strongly that pleasure really is intrinsically desirable. There is a Christian tradition that has certainly assumed it to be so in the way some Christians evangelise. They hold out hopes of heaven where there is no pain, freedom from guilt, plenty of joy and some offer a gospel of prosperity here on earth. They are offers of pleasure to be found in Jesus Christ in this life and the next.

An appeal to the greatest good for the greatest number is an appeal to our human nature and the intrinsic value we place on pleasure. Jeremy Bentham, in the eighteenth century, appealed to this part of our humanity by commenting on the contrary suggestion that pleasure is to be avoided and pain something to be sought – what he called the 'principle of asceticism'. His comment was, 'The principle of asceticism never was, nor ever can be, consistently pursued by any living creature. Let but one tenth part of the inhabitants of this earth pursue it consistently, and in a day's time they will have turned it into hell.' It has been suggested that the Puritan suspicion of pleasurable activities came very close to turning life into a hell!

Mrs Thompson also worked on a principle of maximising pleasure and minimising pain, but it was her pleasure and her pain. The consequence of making it individual is that it seems to justify the behaviour of sadistic people who get their own pleasure by inflicting pain on others. In Miss Argyle's opinion such behaviour is morally indefensible. It is wrong to cause pain and to take pleasure in so doing. Sadistic pleasure has to be seen in the fuller picture of the pain that is inflicted.

Classical Utilitarianism

The classical form of utilitarianism seeks the greatest good for the greatest number, where the good is happiness or pleasure. It entails maximising pleasure and minimising pain. An example of the use of these criteria is to be found in the way in which Barry reacted on one occasion when Sophie wondered if they doing the right thing in seeking to have a baby together. His answer was that it was all right as long as John did not know and so no one got hurt. In other words, there would be an increase in the pleasure and happiness of those concerned, including John, and as long as he and Sophie could handle the situation, there would be a minimum of pain.

Politicians often speak as utilitarians, with their claims to seek the good of the whole nation. They speak of having to make 'hard decisions', which signals the need for pain. Yet it is the painful cuts in resources or services which will lead to an increase in happiness and the 'feel-good' factor, right across society at large. To the extent that we accept their arguments, we accept a utilitarian point of view. It may be instrumental – no gain without pain – but it is an example of classical utilitarianism in public life which is long-standing. Bentham (1748–1832) and John Stuart Mill (1806–73), who are both acknowledged as leading utilitarians, were both political and social reformers who saw this ethical theory as the way ahead for public service.

There is a major problem in this, though. How do we measure the amount of pleasure over against pain? Here Bentham and Mill differed. Bentham claimed that it is the **quantity of pleasure** that is the measure. He even produced a calculus to enable us to determine the quantity of pleasure. He proposed that different activities that please should be compared and evaluated by asking such questions as, 'How long will the pleasure last?' 'How intense is it?' 'How many aspects of life does it cover?' 'How certain is the pleasure or is it just a vague possibility?' 'Is the pleasure free from pain or does it entail a little pain?' 'Is the pleasure immediate or does it lie a long way in the future?'

It was on the basis of these kinds of questions that Bentham claimed that pushpin (a child's game) is as good as poetry. In our terms the comparison could be between bingo and poetry. Looked at quantitatively, tabloid newspapers may give more pleasure and hence have more value than the broadsheets, and in the church, family services may have more value than cathedral services for the same reason.

Mill, on the other hand, made a distinction between higher (mental) and lower (bodily) pleasures. This enabled him to argue that the **measure of pleasure is to be found in its quality** rather than its quantity. The result is his view that 'it is better to be a human being dissatisfied than a pig satisfied. Better to be a Socrates dissatisfied than a fool satisfied.'

Bentham's preference for quantity is the more obvious measure, and difficult as it may be to implement, it seems truer to the idea of maximising pleasure. On the other hand, Mill is more attractive to those who take an intellectual approach to life. He placed mental pleasure above bodily pleasure and it has been argued that this is a step that adds a further element to the equation: he seems to be no longer looking at the sheer pleasure of happiness. Perhaps we have to be able to enjoy the pleasures of both mind and body, in order to measure the qualitative differences.

Act Utilitarianism. You may recall that Miss Argyle took the view that a lot of good had come from what Sophie and Barry did, and hence she cautioned Mr Jones to leave things as they were. If John should find out the truth, then it could be different. A philosopher would probably describe Miss Argyle as an **act utilitarian**. That is to say, she viewed this particular case on its own merits, in its own context. She certainly did not appeal to any rules or ask what would happen if everyone did it.

An example of another person who took Miss Argyle's position was the chief priest, Caiaphas, who was involved in the death of Jesus. When the religious leaders met to discuss what to do about the increasing popularity of Jesus and the likely response of the occupying Romans, he said, 'You do not realise that it is better for you that one man die for the people than that the whole nation perish' (John 11:49). Miss Argyle may well have been surprised to find herself sharing her ethics with such a man!

The problem with this position is that it may result in some disturbing situations. For example, it may be that in a given situation a government may decide that vocal dissidents should be shot. The result may be a settled country in which disharmony and violence are significantly reduced and people feel more secure and able to enjoy a more fulfilling way of life. We may conclude that if the end result is the greater happiness of the greater number, then the deaths were morally justified. Or again, a programme of forced sterilisation in a heavily populated country may result in a better standard of living for that population. As act utilitarians we might then think the sterilisation is justified. One of the arguments used by the Nazis to justify their anti-Semitism was the claim that the Jews were the cause of much of the country's economic problem. A more subtle way in which act utilitarianism can be used is in identifying potential criminals and ensuring that they are caused pain and harassment before they actually commit a crime.

The problem in all these cases is one of justice for the victim. Ought dissidents to be killed simply because they disagree with a government? Do the poor who are sterilised have any rights when it is decided to sterilise them, even though the overall amount of happiness is increased? Ought any race to suffer prejudice simply because the majority of people in a country believe they will have a better life without them? If we accept this theory, we may be able to justify the ends, but we are faced with the morality of how we achieve them. There may be moral questions about the means as well as the ends.

Rule Utilitarianism. Utilitarianism does not have to be like this, though. Rather than adopting act utilitarianism we could be **rule utilitarians**. That is to say that we will make our moral decisions on the basis of rules that we accept. This may seem like a return to a form of rule-governed ethics, where there is something intrinsically right or wrong which the rule covers. But **for a utilitarian the rules would be selected by asking what would promote an ultimately intrinsic goal**. We could, for example, agree together to live by the rule that we will try to respect truth telling. The reason we accept it is not that there is something intrinsically good about truth telling. It is that our experience suggests that truth telling tends to promote pleasure. Our experience also tells us that once we start telling lies we very often find ourselves caught in a web of lies and deceits that cause pain. If we are rule utilitarians, then, we will want to live by that rule, and although there may be times when we are tempted to forsake it, we know that in general it will lead to good consequences.

When Jesus was talking to his disciples about love for our enemies, he gave the Golden Rule, 'Do to others as you would have them do to you' (Luke 6:31). It could be part of a rule utilitarian approach to ethics, and we could claim that such a policy is a good rule to follow because it leads to peace and harmony. In this case, though, if we read the context in which Jesus spoke the words, they are clearly part of a way of love that does not seek returns and desirable ends. It is a good example of the difference between the two uses of rules.

We have noticed a number of reasons why a theory that looks

to the consequences of an action does not always have support from those who think about ethical issues:

- There may be cases in which it justifies diminishing the importance of principles such as liberty and justice and clashes with the feeling that many of us have that such principles are of more importance than the consequences.

- We have problems in knowing with any certainty what will generate pleasure or happiness, or even what pleasure is. It is obvious that there are times when we think we are doing things to get pleasure from them only to find that what we achieve is still not what we want. We may give our children expensive toys only to find they are happier playing with a box.

- The real problem is that a theory which looks to the future – what will happen if we do this or that? – always faces the possibility that the future, just because it is the future, will not be as we anticipate it will be.

Nevertheless, despite the difficulties, there is something in the theory that appeals to our desire to achieve a better life or to do what is good, however we define it. It is worth repeating that although many of us may not want to follow a theory that looks to the unknown future, we recognise that what happens to others is an important element in our decision making. The difference is, though, that a person who believes that acts are right or wrong in themselves apart from the consequences, and who takes note of what will happen if a particular line of action is followed, will be looking at the acts to decide how to behave. Following a theory based on the consequences of our actions, we will be looking to the good consequences of the acts because they are good consequences.

In the first part of this chapter we thought about some ways of avoiding an appeal to rules and principles while still accepting that it is the act itself that makes an action right or wrong. We looked specifically at intuitionism and existentialist ethics. Then we turned our attention to a number of further ways of deciding right from wrong:

- Intentions – which look to the future
- Consequences as the criterion for making decisions
- The idea of the greatest good of the greatest number
- The greatest good as pleasure:
    —individual acts that give pleasure
    —rules that lead to pleasure

We have now looked at a number of major ideas that have been raised when thinking about moral obligations, some of which are easily recognisable as influencing the ways in which we make our moral decisions. Many of the positions we have considered are attractive. Some may seem to reflect the religious or political beliefs that we have. We may find that some of them seem to be taught in the Bible, and to that extent we may want to say they are Christian positions on ethics. We may find that in practice we use one or more of them in the way we handle moral issues. We can apply them to our own situations and they give us tools with which we can, in general, cope with moral questions.

With such a range of alternatives, some of which work very well for us, it is no wonder that we disagree about the way we should make decisions, and even more about what we take to be right and wrong, even when we claim to come from the same religious starting point. Diversity does not thereby mean that anything is acceptable and every position is as good as the next. The question still remains as to which view, if any, is a consistent view to hold in the context of the Christian faith. In the following chapters we will look at the ways in which Christian ethics shares some features with non-Christian ethics before we think about some of the distinctive features that make it a Christian ethic. Before this, though, we will look at two writers who have quite different views of Christian ethics to see how they respond to the range of options we have been thinking about in this and the previous chapter.

3

Two Christians and Ethical Theories

We have been looking at a number of ways in which we go about making sense of our need to distinguish right from wrong. Obviously there are significant differences that affect the way we view situations and decide on what ought to be done.

Christians share that need to distinguish right from wrong, and in doing so they reflect the same concerns as the society in which they live. But they also have an important interest because they hold that God's perfection includes a perfection in his knowledge of what is right and wrong. If following God involves the whole of life, and that is their belief, then it includes following his form of moral life. Morality, then, is a very live issue for them and indeed living a morally good life is expected of them. One of the consequences of this expectation is that when society begins to feel some concern about the moral standards in society, the Church is likely to be accused of not giving a moral lead.

In the previous chapters we have been thinking about some of the approaches people have found useful in taking moral decisions. In this chapter we will look at two accounts of ethics in which Christians have used the sort of approaches we have been looking at.

Even though Christians agree on many things, they are like the rest of society in that they do not always agree on the way they should take their moral decisions, even though traditionally they are thought to agree on some form of a rule-based ethic. In practice there are Christians who find what they think is a Christian position from almost anywhere in the range of recognised options, and some may even have their very own approach that does not match anything we have been looking at! To give some idea of how the main lines of thought have been viewed by Christians, we are going to look at the ideas of two writers who, in the second part of this century, have been influential in provoking people to think about the nature of Christian ethics.

Joseph Fletcher

When *Situation Ethics*, written by Joseph Fletcher, was published in 1966, it proved to be extremely provocative. It appeared at a time when the Church was facing a major challenge to its traditional ideas from the theology of John Robinson, popularised in his book *Honest To God*. *Situation Ethics* appeared to be in the same radical mould, a view that seemed to be confirmed when John Robinson called Fletcher's ideas 'the only ethic for "man come of age"'. The result was one of rejection and hostility among traditional Christian thinkers, but Fletcher was established as an important force to be reckoned with in the field and his work came to be seen as a significant part of any serious discussion of Christian ethics.

For some of his critics Fletcher is the epitome of a liberal approach to ethics that does not even warrant the label of 'Christian'. In his defence it must be said that at times he has not always been fairly represented, and it is often people who hear about some of the suggested implications of his ideas rather than the arguments he uses to support them, who respond most strongly.

The problem for many is that Fletcher seems to be quite unprincipled and to open the way for any form of behaviour to be acceptable as long as it can be seen as an expression of love, but this is to miss the point of what he is saying. He is not saying that anything goes. Indeed, he is firmly against any such idea that would claim that ethics can be reduced to decisions taken solely by reference to the particular action on a particular occasion. As such he is certainly not suggesting any form of existential ethics.

In this respect he joins forces with the apostle Paul in totally rejecting the idea that any sort of behaviour whatsoever is acceptable. Paul found this idea among those who understood their new-found Christian faith to mean that they were no longer subject to the demands of the Law. The argument was that as they were now under grace rather than Law, the moral demands of the old dispensation no longer applied. Paul had to correct such ideas and one of his major responses is in Romans 6, where he writes, 'What shall we say, then? Shall we go on sinning, so that grace may increase? By no means! We died to sin; how can we live in it any longer?' To be under grace rather than Law does not mean that there are no constraints in moral life. Paul had to fight against such antinomianism, as this teaching is called, and in this century Fletcher has followed him in his condemnation of such views.

At the other extreme Fletcher puts the ethics of legalism. The Christian tradition has, in Fletcher's view, been legalistic and he rejects this too. Just as the Jewish tradition of living by the Law has its rules, so it has been paralleled in the history of the Christian Church. The Church has followed its Old Testament precedents and formed its own rules and 'laws' which define what is right and wrong behaviour. He claims that although Protestantism has avoided intricate law codes, it has nevertheless become bound by a rigidity which results from requiring rules to guide moral life. To put it in the terms that we met when thinking about Mr Jones, Fletcher rejects a rule-governed deontology, and it may be that the strength of reaction by some of his Christian critics arises in part from this rejection of a moral code made up of specific rules. His views certainly go against a very strong tradition in the Christian Church.

If Christian ethics is not about the licence of antinomianism, nor about the legalism of a rule-based deontology, what has Fletcher to offer? His response to these extremes is to take a more moderate position that he describes as **situation ethics**.

Briefly, this means that **we have to approach each new situation where a moral decision is required, with a commitment to act in love, or to judge what is happening in the light of love**. Of course, it is unlikely that any two situations will be exactly the same, and that means that we have to apply this overarching principle of love to each new case. As Fletcher describes it, 'The situationist follows a moral law or violates it according to love's need.' No action contains within itself the quality of right or wrong, but all have to be viewed in the context of the situation, with all the factors involved, in order that love may be shown.

This means, of course, that we may have to do some work in deciding what the loving act would be in a given situation, and that is accepted. If we accept this view of ethics, we have no option but to take decisions, for there is no way of automatically reading off what the loving thing is in each and every case. We still have to decide what is the loving thing to do.

It is wrong to think that this means that Fletcher is rejecting all other principles. Far from rejecting them, he argues that the Christian situationist's approach is to follow the maxims and principles that are part of his heritage and of the conventions of his community. However, the point is that they are not to be binding in all situations. Their role is to give illumination rather than lay down decrees to be obeyed. He can follow them and take advantage of the insights they provide, but with the proviso that they are not seen as absolutes. **The only compelling command and principle is love** and if it is necessary in a given situation, the maxims and principles are to be laid aside where they conflict with the interests of love.

There are no commands or principles whatsoever which cannot be laid aside, except the command to love. He makes the observation that in classic moral theology the normal procedure is to 'follow laws but do it *as much as* possible according to love and according to reason'. On the other hand, situationists reverse the relative weight of law and love and place laws in a subservient position, with love as the all-important requirement. It is easy to see why Fletcher has been so badly received in some sections of the Church.

In terms of the ethical theories we have previously met, Fletcher is certainly not advocating a rule-governed ethic. Rather, he has a theory of moral obligation in which he looks at the consequences of actions to decide whether they are right or wrong. In his view there is a single goal to be reached: love. He follows the principle of the greatest good of the greatest number, but rather than seeing pleasure as the greatest good, he replaces it with *agape*: self-giving love. At the same time, to achieve the greatest good of love for the greatest number is an absolute moral command, which becomes a duty laid on those who recognise its truth and want to follow a Christian way.

If we become a little more technical, then we have to say that his teleological theory is not a form of rule utilitarianism, in which there are rules or principles which will promote love. His approach is more that of an act utilitarian for whom each situation requires a fresh examination and a new decision to be made on the basis of love. When thinking about act utilitarianism earlier we could well have mentioned situation ethics as a distinctive form of that position.

There is a clue as to the particular way Fletcher wants us to use utilitarianism, in the way he looks at the incident in Mark 14:3–9 in which the writer tells of a woman coming to Jesus in Bethany where she broke a jar of expensive perfume and poured the contents on the head of Jesus. Some of those who saw the incident were indignant at what they thought was a waste, 'It could be sold for more than a year's wages and the money given to the poor.' This is an example of utilitarians at work, wanting the benefits to spread as widely as possible. Jesus, on the other hand, said that she had done a beautiful thing.

Fletcher sides with the utilitarians and, given his views, it is a consistent position to take. It is an understandable response to the incident if we see the greatest good in terms of quantity. With all that money available from the sale, without a doubt, a great many people could have been helped. Over against that is the benefit to a single person: Jesus. Jesus's response was to say that the woman had done a beautiful thing to him, and it was a preparation for his burial. Perhaps we need to look not so much at the **quantity** of benefit, which seems to be the criterion that Fletcher uses, but to look at the **quality** of love that was expressed.

So far we have looked at Fletcher in the light of the theory of ethics. We get a better view of what he is really advocating when we consider some of his examples. He tells the story of the ship, *William Brown*, which hit an iceberg in 1841, and began to sink. One of the boats that got away was under the command of the mate, but in all it contained forty people: twice what the boat was intended to take. With that many people on board they were likely to be swamped and all would be drowned, so the mate ordered most of the men into the sea, and when they refused, one of the seamen named Holmes threw them overboard. The survivors in the boat were eventually picked up, and Holmes was charged with murder. Fletcher contrasts the approach of traditional Christian ethics with that of situation ethics when he says that if we start with what he calls legalism – a rule-based ethic that sees right and wrong to be inherent in the deed – we would say that Holmes did an evil thing, even if there were extenuating circumstances. Situation ethics says that Holmes did a good thing.

It is easy to see that the situationist has to face the problem that is part of any ethical theory that seeks the good of the greatest number, namely, the place of the individual in the overall scheme. What do we say about the men who were thrown from the lifeboat?

Take another case. In 1945 the Allies had available the first atomic bomb. Harry Truman, the President of the United States, was faced with the responsibility of deciding whether or not to use it. A committee was set up to consider both if and how to use it. Understandably opinions differed. Some opposed its use altogether. Others were in favour. Still others thought that the Japanese ought to be told what they could expect. In the end it was the decision of the president, and it is a matter of history that the bomb was dropped. Fletcher calls the decision one made on the basis of a vast 'agapeic calculus'. In other words, the president had to weigh up what was the most loving thing to do. That sounds strange in view of the horror, the loss of life that was involved, and the future fear that the bomb has caused. But it has to be seen in the context of the lives that would have been lost if the war had continued with conventional weapons, and it was the job of the president to weigh up all the factors involved. No doubt he had lived the whole of his life with the principle that life was precious and the taking of it was not a light matter. That would have been a relevant principle. But in the eyes of a situationist the decision had to go beyond that. A decision on what love required had to be taken there and then with the information that was available. It has since been suggested that perhaps the Japanese were nearing the point of surrender anyway, but situation ethics is realistic in so far as it accepts the here and now as the context in which to decide. On reflection there may have been other options but the situationist has to work with what he has got. The incident is a good example of situation ethics at work.

Obviously, love in such cases is not a matter of liking or of being sentimental about the people concerned. There was no room for that kind of love in Truman's decision. But for situation ethics that is the way it is. The situationist takes a seemingly hard line in these situations. The need is for cool, calculating appraisals that get beyond selfish or soft interests. Christian love is about loving the unlovable and the unliked, and to pretend otherwise is to miss the nature of love. Fletcher quotes Paul's words to the Romans, 'Christ died for the ungodly . . . But God demonstrates his own love for us in this: While we were still sinners, Christ died for us' (Romans 5:6, 8). The passage goes on to point out that at the time when we were reconciled to God we were his enemies. Love is not about inner feelings. It is the **work** of love rather than a **feeling** of love that matters, and that work is done without looking for any return. Christian love is not reciprocal. It is not a mutual arrangement.

A further feature of Fletcher's ethic is the way in which, in contrast to Kant and much of our instinctive belief, he accepts that the ends justify the means. He says, 'Unless some purpose or end is in view, to justify or sanctify it, any action we take will be literally meaningless – i.e. means-less, accidental, merely random, pointless.'

One of the most quoted of Fletcher's illustrations raises the matter in a way that is startling for many Western Christians because it challenges traditional sexual ethics: a particularly sensitive area. The story is one of four cases with which the book ends. They are there to help us think about the ideas contained in the book, and hence Fletcher does not comment on them.

This particular story concerns Mrs Bergmeier, who was a German woman taken prisoner by the Russians during their drive into Germany towards the end of the Second World War. She was unable to get news to anyone to say what had happened before she was taken off to the Ukraine to a prison camp. At that time her husband was also in a prisoner-of-war camp in Wales, so their three children were left to fend for themselves. When her husband returned to Berlin he spent weeks looking for them but eventually found them and was able to gather the family together again, even though none of them knew what had happened to their mother. It soon became clear that she was very much needed to draw the family together again.

In her camp, Mrs Bergmeier heard that the family were looking for her, but there were only two grounds on which prisoners could be released from that particular camp. One was in cases of illness for which there was no treatment in the camp, but that release usually meant being transferred to another camp. The second ground was in cases of pregnancy, in which case the woman would be returned to Germany. After much heart-searching she asked a guard to impregnate her and in due time she was returned to Berlin and her family, carrying a child. The story is that she was received home with welcome arms and when little Dietrich was born they all loved him for bringing them together as a family. Fletcher finishes the story by asking some questions. Should they feel grateful to the guard? Had Mrs Bergmeier done the right thing? We are left to decide.

The incident starkly poses the problem many have with situationism. Do the ends justify the means? On the basis of the claims of situation ethics the answer is 'yes'. In the eyes of those who advocate such an ethic, the fact there was an act of adultery is irrelevant when the goal is the expression of love. The morality of the means used is seen as being dependent on whether or not the end result will be an expression of love.

Clearly, Joseph Fletcher presents difficulties for those who have a more traditional Christian ethic which is about the observance of a moral code. Even for those who take a view of ethics in terms of consequences, there is something ruthlessly logical about the way in which he argues his case and the conclusions he draws. For our immediate purposes, though, the interest is in the way in which he handles the theories we were earlier trying to understand.

John Murray

It was in 1957 that John Murray's book *Principles of Conduct* first appeared, since when it has been through a number of reprints. It is a book that has the subtitle *Aspects of Biblical Ethics* which describes its emphasis, but that is not to say that Murray shares the belief of some Christians that biblical and Christian ethics can be separated and that the two are not the same thing. Murray rejects any such distinction. To talk of biblical ethics is to talk of Christian ethics.

While Fletcher has something in common with those who look to the consequences of actions to make their moral judgments, Murray takes a totally different point of view. He would have approved of the stance which Mr Jones took towards the conduct of Sophie. Murray's ethic is essentially one of living by rules, for in his view the essence of ethics is the observance of God's commands or precepts as they are found in the Bible.

It is interesting that Murray has nothing to say about the role of the consequences of our actions. The consequences are not a consideration. He does have something to say about motives, and here he picks up what Fletcher sees as the core of Christian ethics: love. It is love for God and the people around us that motivates and carries into effect the Law of God. This is in sharp contrast with Fletcher, for Murray holds that the role of love is *only* that of motivating our behaviour. He does not see love as being the measure of what is right or wrong, for love does not determine what is morally right and wrong: it is about motive, not the content of moral life.

There is more to Christian behaviour than just acting out of love. Far from being the final court of appeal in our decision making, love is but a part of a much wider consideration. The reason he takes this view of the place of love is that to love is to obey God's commands. The apostle John's words, 'This is love for God: to obey his commands' (1 John 5:3) are significant for Murray, for to love is to obey the commandments. It is because of this that Murray claims that obeying the commandments of God is at the heart of Christian ethics. The confirmation of this is said to be in the fact that love itself is commanded by Jesus. To love is also to obey Jesus. **Obedience to rules, then, is the nature of Christian ethics, for biblical commandments are the norms of our behaviour**. How he would have supported Mr Jones!

When we ask what these commandments are that Christians ought to keep, Murray uses the language of law, as we might expect. He rejects the idea that Christians are bound to the rites and ceremonial laws of the Old Testament, but posits rather that they are bound to the Law of God and of Christ because they are committed to God. What might this Law be? The answer is the Ten Commandments. They constitute a sufficient set of precepts to guide us because they underlie other law statements in both the Old and New Testaments. Murray refers to the lists of sins that Paul gives in passages such as 1 Corinthians 6:9–10 and points out that they are all forms of rejection of the Ten Commandments.

The way in which he applies his insistence on the centrality of the Ten Commandments can be seen in the context of his views on moral principles. When Murray talks about law and rules he means just that. Most of those who follow a rule-governed ethic accept that the rules in the Bible do not cover every situation in which we have to make decisions. They accept that there is a need to have some underlying principles as well, and Christians who think this way claim that those principles can be found in the Bible. Murray rejects such talk of principles and he uses an example from the New Testament to explain why. In 1 Corinthians 8, Paul refers to some in the church who had a problem with the idea of eating meat which had been offered to idols. He recommends that the church abstain from eating such meat in order that the matter should not become a stumbling block to the weak. One explanation of the passage is to say that it is an example of the principle of love being applied in the church. Murray's comment is that it is true that there is no law against eating such meat, because idols are meaningless as there is only one God, so the meat is not contaminated by being offered up to an idol.

Why then should they not eat it? Not because love dictates it. Murray's argument is that to imply that an idol has some significance by assuming it affects meat which has been offered to it, is to break the first commandment, 'You shall have no other gods before me.' To abstain from eating such meat, then, is not because the principle of love applies but to stop running the risk of the weaker brethren even raising the possibility that the idol means something. The issue is not one of applying a principle, but of helping someone keep the first commandment. It is to enable that person to keep the Law. Love, then, is not abstracted from the Law but is itself commanded and is part of its content. For Murray there are no principles to be applied, only commands to be obeyed.

Murray has a rule-governed view of ethics and the rules are the Ten Commandments. But that leaves us with the question of dealing with difficult cases where two commandments seem to conflict. For example, one of the situations that Fletcher raises is that of the way in which deceit and lies are used in war in order to mislead the enemy. In Fletcher's view that is acceptable where it is the most loving thing to do, given the overall context. Murray has another view. He considers the occasion when Joshua and the Israelite army were trying to capture the town of Ai (Joshua 8). The strategy that Joshua used was for some of his army to retreat when the men of Ai came out to fight. As they fled his men led their enemies into an ambush set for them. The question Murray poses is whether this is acceptable in view of the deceit that was being employed.

Murray holds that the action was not deceitful. He speaks of the assumption that for us to be truthful we must ensure that the hearers understand what is being said and have all the relevant facts that we have. His argument is that this is a false requirement. If others misunderstand and misrepresent what we say and do, that is their problem and we are not responsible if we have spoken truthfully. The men of Ai were simply ignorant of some of the facts that Joshua had when his men fled. Murray says that it is our responsibility to act and speak in the light of all the data and consideration we have. If we do that we are not guilty of lying. How it is heard is not our problem.

This way of proceeding is not unusual. In effect it means that in cases of telling the truth, for example, it involves only telling part of the truth, a practice sometimes followed by politicians! Alternatively, it would be acceptable to tell the truth in such an ambiguous way that the hearer will hear what they want to hear rather than the truth. It is not a case of lying, but it is not a case of making the truth plain either. Murray is not alone in advocating this. There is a long tradition of using this ploy. William Ames, a Puritan leader in the days of Elizabeth I, wrote, 'It is sometimes lawful, so long as truth is not violated, to utter words from which in all probability the hearers will draw a false inference. This is not lying, nor false witness, but merely giving others an opportunity of making a mistake, with a view not to their commiting sin, but rather to their avoiding it.'

Ames has a good intention in mind and it is this that justifies it. Some people do the same thing when wanting to shield others from a truth that will hurt or even damage them, for example, not giving bad news about their life expectancy: the intentions are good.

Notice, though, that the same move can be made to avoid taking responsibility for our acts. 'Were you near the scene of the crime in that town last Thursday?' 'I was nowhere near that town.' But if the truth were really told the suspect meant he was nowhere near during the rest of the week.

It is also sometimes used where the intentions are not good at all. In a television play by Dennis Potter, one of the characters was a travelling salesman. In one scene he was in a car with a woman he had met, and she asked, 'Are you married?' His answer was, 'Do I look as though I am married?' which she took to mean that he was single. It was a deliberately ambiguous reply that kept open the possibility of what the salesman hoped would be an illicit relationship.

In Sophie's story Mr Jones believed that moral judgments are decided by the action itself and not about consequences or intentions. John Murray has a similar view. He uses a general ethical approach in a way that is more consistent than is usual. He comes to his position from his Christian beliefs and, in particular, from his high view of the Scriptures, and in so doing he offers us a clear and consistent example of a rule-governed ethic.

The two positions we have considered are very different, as Figure 3.1 shows (see overleaf).

We have looked at two Christian writers who have adopted general ethical positions which are, in principle, used by men and women from a variety of religious and ideological points of view. Whether Joseph Fletcher and John Murray are right in claiming that they are presenting Christian approaches to ethics is open to question. Certainly, their views are so different

Figure 3.1

Fletcher		*Murray*
Love	**keyword**	Obedience
Greatest good of the greatest number	**type of ethic**	A rule-based ethic
No action has within itself the quality of right or wrong	**premise**	There are right actions and wrong actions
Love	**absolutes**	The Ten Commandments

that it is unlikely that either of them could acknowledge that the other was true to the Christian gospel. This difference is the outstanding feature to notice. We might have expected two men who start from a belief in the Christian God would have agreed on an ethical position but this is not the case. Later in the book we will see some of the reasons why this is so.

We are now going to proceed to think further about Christian ethics, but this time in relation to other ethical positions.

4

Christian and Secular Similarities

When Mr Jones was struggling to know what to do about Sophie's adultery he must have wished that there was only one way of coming to moral decisions. Then life would have been so much simpler for him. Instead, he found people reacting in different ways.

Taking decisions concerning what is right and wrong is obviously something about which people disagree in the broad approaches they take. If that appears to make ethics complicated, it becomes even more so when those who accept that it has to do with rules for living disagree among themselves, as do those who think it is about the consequences of our actions. The result is that there is a variety of approaches that are seriously held to be correct, from which we can choose.

With so many alternative positions available, is it possible to say that there is one that is correct for all human beings? That is a big question. To be more specific and less ambitious, is there one way that best characterises Christian ethics? Is it essentially similar to one of the positions we have already met, as Fletcher and Murray would seem to suggest is possible, or is it best described in some other way? Or perhaps there is nothing distinctive about Christian ethics and the word 'Christian' in this context is redundant. This would fit in with the view that all ethical positions are of equal worth because they have facets that people can accept as being valid insights into morality. We might then go further and say that they are all Christian approaches because the good God is the source of all that is true and right. This is to make a theological point, but unfortunately it does not help to answer our questions about what is morally right and wrong.

Later in the book we will see that there are some features of a Christian ethic that makes it distinctive from non-Christian ethics. But before we look at these distinctive elements it is well to realise that there are also some features of Christian ethics that are shared with other groups. In this chapter we will begin to put Christian ethics into context by thinking about some of these common features.

Better or the Same?

One way in which Christians sometimes claim that their ethic is different is to appeal to the content of the moral Christian life. For example, they sometimes say that non-Christian ethics, whether religious or non-religious, do not have such high standards as a Christian ethic. Such a claim may be true, but there are three points to note before we accept it.

First, **the claim is so sweeping that it is virtually impossible to substantiate**. To do that would mean examining the moral beliefs and practices of countless groups around the world, making an unbiased evaluation, and then comparing them with Christianity. A hard task!

Second, **we would need to compare like with like**. We are all likely to compare the best of our tradition with the worst of our rivals, or alternatively we are prone to compare the ideals of our own position with the practices of others. We might point the finger at religions that have practised child sacrifice and say how much worthier is a Christian morality that rejects such a thing. We point to the part played by Christians in the growth of education and in caring for the dying, in the abolition of slavery and child labour in Britain. We might cite the high view that Christianity takes of marriage and the good things it has done to bring a better standard of life to men and women throughout the world. Yet if we are to use such things to say that Christians have high moral standards, we have to see what good things other groups have done over the years.

We also have to acknowledge that there is another side to the conduct of Christians. The way Christians have behaved and do behave, and the things done in the name of Christ through the centuries and in our own day is, in many instances, a cause of shame. Christians talk about following the Prince of Peace, but they have a history of violence and sectarianism. The Crusades and the Inquisition are examples of Christians being cruel in their zeal for the truth. Some conversions to Christianity have been the result of coercion or bribery. Disputes between Christians have cost lives. Different groups who seek to follow Christ refuse to acknowledge each other because they do not agree on matters of theology. Christians have been known to hound those with whom they disagree on matters of doctrine. Apartheid was supported by some Christian groups. Part of the tragedy of so much that is unacceptable is that it has been in the name of Christ. We need to compare theory with theory and practice with practice – the good, the bad and the indifferent.

Third, **if we are looking solely at the content of Christian morality, it is not obvious that there is much difference between Christian and non-Christian groups**. It is a matter of fact that people do not need a Christian faith in order to behave in a morally acceptable way. We only have to look around us to see it. Caring and considerate people are to be found right across society, among those with a religious faith and those without any faith. Their actions in every part of their lives are not always precisely those expected of the Christian community (neither are those within that community!), but many without a faith in the Christian God do share the same values, and at times show them more clearly and consistently than Christians. It is often among the non-Christian members of society that we see compassion, a respect for human beings, a desire to see that justice is done and a willingness and ability to make things happen. They run charities. They use the media to make us all aware of the evils that are in the world, and they change society for good – internationally, nationally and locally. To suggest that there are no morally good people outside the Church just does not bear serious consideration.

The apostle Paul appears to have seen people outside the Church behaving in morally acceptable ways in his time. In his letter to the Romans he writes about those without a knowledge of the Law doing 'by nature things required by the law, they are a law for themselves, even though they do not have the law, since they show that the requirements of the law are written on their hearts, their consciences also bearing witness, and their thoughts now accusing, now even defending them' (Romans 2:14–15). In other words, there is something about human beings that gives them a knowledge of what is right and wrong, and the moral standard is that which a good Jew like Paul, steeped in Old Testament teaching, could recognise and accept. Maybe the moral code of some people is not as fully developed as some Christians would wish and it may not always agree in detail with what Christians might prefer to see, but it is there.

Biblical Standards of Morality

Christians sometimes claim that their moral code is unique because it is to be found in the Bible. We have to be careful about such claims. The ethical requirements of the Old Testament did not simply appear out of the blue in the form in which we know them. Although a superficial reading of Exodus might suggest that the prohibitions in the second part of the Ten Commandments were suddenly given specifically for Israel, it is not so. People already knew that some ways of behaving were wrong long before they were put into the form of the Commandments. Scholars tell us that both the moral and legal content of the laws given to Israel, when they wandered in the wilderness, have parallels in the records we have of other semi-nomadic groups in the area. They are not a unique set of rules for living, but reflect a common way of life in the Near East and are not specifically Israelite at all. It means that they were not just the ways of behaving that were appropriate for God's chosen people, Israel.

When we turn to the New Testament we find the same thing. The ethical requirements we find in the letters of Church leaders like Peter and Paul did not simply appear as Christian precepts distinct from the moral life of the rest of the Graeco-Roman world of the time. Paul and the other leaders of the Church did not sit down and work out what would be appropriate for the Church. In general, New Testament moral teaching matched what was commonly expected of a morally upright citizen of the time. Having said that, there is one notable point at which Paul's values were distinct from those of the Greeks of the time, and it arose from the way in which he centred his ethics on Jesus Christ. Paul encouraged his friends to show humility. In his eyes it was a virtue to be prized because Jesus, whom he served, humbled himself and took the form of a servant. Such an idea was in contrast to the Greek views at the time. For the Greeks, humility was not a positive virtue at all, and the idea of prizing it would have been startling for many of Paul's converts. At the same time, what would have been strange to the Greeks was very familiar to the Jews of Paul's day.

There were other virtues that Paul encouraged that were very common in Greek thought. For example, Philippians 4:8 reads, 'Finally brothers, whatever is true, whatever is noble, whatever is right, whatever is pure, whatever is lovely, whatever is admirable – if anything is excellent or praiseworthy – think about such things.' The items Paul lists are rare in his letters, but they were very familiar to Greek thought – indeed, it has been suggested that this verse could well have been used as a summary of Greek ethics.

Another example is in what Martin Luther called the 'household codes' in Ephesians 5:22–6:9; Colossians 3:18–4:1 and 1 Peter 2:18–3:7, where both Paul and Peter wrote about different sorts of relationship: wives and husbands, children and parents, slaves and masters. This sort of teaching is also to be found in Greek circles. The New Testament use of it does not match the

Greek version exactly, and Paul certainly added to what was already there, but it strongly suggests that he was drawing on teaching that was already in existence.

It is also worth noting that there are places in Paul's letters which contain suggestions that his readers would already know what was the right way to behave, and that they should get on and do it. When he wrote, 'whatever is admirable – if anything is excellent or praiseworthy' it seems that he is saying that the list he has given is not complete, but if his readers learn of other things that were praiseworthy, they ought to do them. That is to say that he recognised that while there were facets of a Christian way of life that were specifically to do with the theology he taught, he also acknowledged that the moral teaching current at the time also had something worthwhile for Christians to embrace. They were to live up to the ideals of their fellow men and women and to be good citizens.

The same conclusion can be drawn from words he wrote to the Galatians. In chapter 5, verse 19 he gave a list of sinful actions: 'Sexual immorality, impurity and debauchery; idolatry and witchcraft; hatred, discord, jealousy, fits of rage, selfish ambition, dissensions, factions and envy; drunkenness, orgies, and the like.' Not only is the list incomplete, 'and the like' suggesting that they would recognise other forms of evil behaviour, but he introduced this list with the words, 'The acts of the sinful nature are obvious.' Why would they be *obvious* sinful actions if they were not known within the Galatian community? He seems to be appealing to commonly accepted ways of behaving known to his readers.

We have to recognise that the evidence ought to make us wary of making strong claims that Christian moral teaching is in some way better than or different from the teachings of non-Christians. The moral teaching of the Bible is not very much different from that of the general views held by others at the time. Similarly, the moral beliefs and practices of Christians through the centuries and in our own time make it hard to see the moral content as being a distinctive characteristic of

Christian ethics. We need to look elsewhere if we are to find what is distinctive about it, but before we do so there are other similarities between Christian and non-Christian ethics that we should notice.

5

Doing Ethics Together

We are looking at the ways in which Christian ethics is like the ethics of non-Christians, and in the previous chapter we looked at the way in which the kind of behaviour expected of Christians is comparable to that of other people. In this chapter we look at another aspect of ethics that Christians share with non-Christians: **the community nature of ethics**.

Community Ethics

If we think about the responses we found among Mr Jones and his friends, we will soon realise that it is unlikely that they made them up for themselves. We are members of communities that shape the way we think about morality. Whether it be by exposure to our parents and their friends who confirm what they tell us, or by being members of school communities, or of the Church, we learn what those groups think are the appropriate ways to behave. It means that **our morality is in some ways determined by the way of life of our communities**. They are the responses to life of different groups, each of which has its own approach to the matter.

Let us make some guesses. Perhaps Mr Jones is an older man who has been taught that there are certain actions that are always wrong in themselves. It may be hard for him to even contemplate that things may be otherwise, for that was how his parents, and the circles within which they moved, thought about ethics. They were not religious but for their generation of middle class people, the Ten Commandments were assumed to be the basic moral rules behind all moral life, and this is what Mr Jones learned as a child. It seems that Mr Jones has never had cause to think that moral life is anything but a series of clear rules for life.

Let us imagine that Mrs Thompson has had a troubled past and that at some point in her life she was badly let down and hurt by someone. The result is a feeling that she needs to look after number one. Given her past experiences we can understand that trusting other people seems to carry the threat of more pain and trouble. Her ethics of self-interest reflects her experience.

Miss Argyle, however, may be influenced by a group of young people whom she meets from time to time to talk about the world's problems. One of their underlying assumptions, which they come back to again and again, is the belief that the world is in such a terrible mess that the only way out of it is to decide what needs to be done and then to do it. It is a time for radical action because it is only by solving world problems, such as overpopulation and food shortages, that there is any hope for the world. Her group may have talked long about the way to solve such problems and decided that there may have to be a lot of pain and unhappy decisions to be taken in the more affluent countries if we are to achieve a tolerable world for the majority of people. That some will be hurt in the process seems to be a small price to pay for the benefits that could be achieved if the world's leaders had enough courage and will to attack the causes of the world's ills.

Terry may be another who is influenced by his friends. Perhaps at university he spends long hours bemoaning the way in which the older generation are careful to be seen in the right light, and so concerned to do the right things that they have lost their integrity. If only people were honest about themselves and their situation. When someone came along and started talking about existentialists like Jean-Paul Sartre, Terry and his friends decided this was the way for them.

All this is speculation but it makes an important point about our moral beliefs. We are not objective in the sense that ethics is just there for us to discover. Our particular way of understanding moral life did not drop from the sky in a form that everyone immediately sees and accepts, but rather the stances we take are determined by our experiences and those of the community of which we are a part. The result is that in a sense there is no such thing as ethics which exists apart from communities. There is only existentialist ethics and humanist ethics and Buddhist ethics and Christian ethics, and many more besides.

Books are written about ethics from particular standpoints, and even within these broad categories of ethics there are sub-categories. For example, within Christian ethics there are books on Anglican ethics and Roman Catholic ethics. When some people start reading about ethics they like to know where the author comes from. Is the book written from a Lutheran or Baptist standpoint, or by an evangelical, or by someone thought to be radical, or by whom? This concern to know the background to books on ethics simply confirms an important recognition that ethics reflects the communities within which it is formed, believed in and practised.

Professional Ethics. The reality is that different groups have their own distinctive values and take ethical positions which control what is right for their members to do and say. This can be seen in professional groups like doctors and lawyers who have their own professional ethics and bodies to see that the appropriate ethical standards are upheld, and from time to time the newspapers carry stories of professional men and women appearing before their professional bodies to answer charges of unprofessional conduct.

The armed services is a good example of a body which is concerned to maintain appropriate standards of behaviour from their personnel. In October 1997 a number of army officers admitted having group sex with a girl but were cleared of a charge of gang rape. Although legally innocent of gang rape the army immediately announced an enquiry into their behaviour as there are certain standards they expect of their officers. Later that same month the army announced a code of conduct which is thought appropriate for those who may have to support each other in battle.

Some churches, too, have professional standards for their clergy. In 1991 the Church of England published a statement by the House of Bishops entitled *Issues in Human Sexuality*, which attracted particular attention for its statements about homosexuality. The report called on homosexuals in the Church to take note of the teaching about sexuality which the report contained, as expressing the Church's teaching about homosexual practices, but recognised that there are those who feel that they have more hope of growing in their love of God and their neighbour by having a lifelong homosexual relationship which is expressed physically. The report acknowledged that the bishops were attempting to cope with the constant tension between a God-given ideal and the freedom of individuals to make their own choices.

If the way that tension is resolved causes problems when it refers to the laity, they are increased when it goes on to talk of the clergy. Whilst the laity were free to ignore the teaching if they so wished, the clergy were given no choice. For them, there are but two options: they can either enter into a heterosexual marriage, or be celibate. They were not given the opportunity to choose how they expressed their sexuality outside these boundaries.

There has been a great deal said about what is seen as an injustice in this. It has been suggested that the same moral standards ought to be applied to all members of the Church, for after all, a Christian is a Christian no matter whether a parson or a layperson. But this is to miss the point. Whatever we may think of same-gender sex, what the bishops were doing was trying to set out something of the conduct to be expected of leaders of the Church. They argued that while it should be possible to accommodate ideals to human need where it will help to maintain a love of God and neighbour, there is a point where the ideal has to be preserved from misrepresentation. The clergy ought to present an example of the ideal being lived out.

Homosexual practice is, if you like, part of the professional ethic of Church leaders, to be put alongside other forms of behaviour deemed inappropriate for those who claim to be teachers of a Christian way of life. It was a statement about what the bishops took to be appropriate practices of such men and women. The report is clear regarding what the bishops think is the appropriate way of exercising sexuality for all Christians, but for the leaders of the Church it is not a matter for choice. Their professional position means some activities are simply unacceptable. It is all part of the ethic of that particular community.

The Community of Faith

Not all churches have the same ideas about what is thought to be appropriate moral behaviour for their members. Some have their own particular ethic. On 10 October 1997, the *Daily Telegraph* reported that the Free Presbyterian Church of Scotland had reprinted in its monthly magazine an article first written in the 1920s. Apparently the article appeared because of reports that members of the Free Church had been seen 'resplendent in Highland dress, cavorting on the dance floor' at a wedding. According to the newspaper report, the article warns that dancing is 'for the frivolous, the empty-headed, the vain, the silly, the dissipated and the dissolute, both men and women'. The newspaper added that a former Lord Chancellor, Lord Mackay, had been forced to leave the Free Presbyterian Church in 1989, after attending two Roman Catholic funerals. Not many other church groups appear to take that particular line, but then they are different communities with different values. The ethics of the Free Presbyterian Church is derived from that particular community of believers and reflects its beliefs and values.

The rights and wrongs of any of these incidents is not our concern, but they reflect the way in which ethics has its base in communities and the values they hold. Whether we claim that our ethics reflect the well-worn approaches of traditional secular ethics, or come from within the Christian tradition, they represent the experiences and understanding of the group from which they emanate. It is the group that sustains them and determines what changes are admissible.

Even when we talk of Christian ethics, we need to bear in mind that there are different Christian groups with different values. That was very obvious when we looked at the writings of Joseph Fletcher and John Murray, but the reason is that they come from quite different communities within the Church. The values of their groups are shaped by the communities and, in turn, these values shape the communities. **Ethics is a community matter and this is true of the Church**. At times it is the wider community of the Church; at other times the more individual ethic of groups within the Church.

An Ethic with a Past

Many people realise that their family has a story. They note the family traditions at special times and events, for example, when there is a birth or death in the family. They probably recognise that they have family traditions at Christmas. There may be a particular ritual about the giving and opening of presents; the family always has to wait until the end of the Queen's speech, and then it is traditional that Uncle John always gives out the presents that are under the tree. He always cracks the same jokes while doing it, and Auntie May tells the same stories every year. Christmas would not be the same without the family traditions. Such things are part of the story of the family that will be passed down to the children when they are old enough to understand.

Some people look for the story of the family's past. They collect photographs and trace their ancestry. They discover where their family originally came from, and where they have lived. They find out what they did for a living and sometimes find there was a family trade. They may well find there was a tradition in the family that they became soldiers, or stonemasons, or doctors, or farmers. It is all part of trying to discover the story of the family. The story is about the history of men and women: the traditions they had, the journeys they made, the identity they made for themselves.

In the same way Christians, as God's people, have a story. They too have traditions and events which have not only formed their way of life as a family, but actually give the family its identity. The story includes the lives and works of those whom we think are good examples of what it means to be God's people. Part of the story of the Christian Church is shared with Jews and together they look to Abraham and Moses, David and Job. In the New Testament Christians look to the apostles and their colleagues, and to the life of the early Church in general, and they note what happened to them, the way they responded and the wisdom they passed on to the next generation.

Jesus is part of that story, though not primarily as a moral teacher: the whole of his life, work, death and resurrection is part of the story. What specific moral teaching he gave came quite incidentally in the course of his everyday relations with the people he met and the situations he faced. In the same way, when the apostle Paul was trying to help the early Church live in a way that was appropriate to the gospel he did it, not by writing ethical textbooks, but by responding to the lives of his friends and the different situations they were facing at the time. It was applied ethics and part of the ongoing story of the Church.

The Bible is the source of the start of the story of God and his people's walk with him. At the centre of it is the story of the person of Jesus Christ who is God incarnate, crucified and resurrected, but the entire biblical story contains within it those values which Christians prize, and Christian views of what is morally good and right are in part a reflection of those values. What is deemed bad or wrong are in contradiction of those values.

Within the Christian story there are substories: plots within plots. Different church groups have their own stories in addition to the one they share with others as Christians. The Methodist story, for example, looks to the Wesleys as showing what it means to live for God in the Methodist way; Cistercians look to their founding fathers – men such as St Bernard and William of Thierry who gave direction to their order; the Church of England has Cranmer as a key figure in their story; Anglo-Catholics look to Newman, Pusey and Keble; while evangelicals may well turn to Calvin, or, in more recent times, to John Stott and Martyn Lloyd-Jones. In all these cases there is a story that is bound up with teaching and events and the distinctive ways of being God's people. From these stories, sometimes lasting centuries, different groups get their identity, which affects the way they worship, the way they relate to the wider community, and also their ethics.

Each of these particular stories is but part of the wider Christian story which finds its focus in the events surrounding Israel, and in Jesus Christ. The story of the Christian community derives from the history of what it means to follow God, which we have in the whole story of God's people through the ages and around the world, and it gives a tradition of the distinctive features of what it means to live as part of that particular community.

Whatever view of ethics we take within the Church, then, a Christian ethic is like that of other groups in that it comes from its community. In the Christian community we note two things. First, ethics involves more than the decisions of synods or diaconates or elders. It comes from the whole community. Second, there are groups within the wider community of faith that form more specific communities.

Common Content – Different Communities

There is an apparent contradiction in what has been said so far. We have seen that whatever it is that makes Christian ethics Christian, it is not its content. For the most part, what counts as right and wrong is the same as that found among other communities. Yet we have also seen that Christian ethics is Christian because it is the expression of the life, beliefs and values of the Christian community. On the one hand, it has been said that the content is the same, but on the other, that it is the expression of the Christian community.

The contradiction is more apparent than real, and that is for two reasons. First, because the *content* of Christian ethics is not unique, it does not follow that there is nothing else that can be distinctive about the Christian community's values and approaches, and we will see that there are indeed other distinctive features.

Second, if men and women of goodwill from different communities seek the best for their society, it is not surprising that they are likely to have common ground about the content of what they believe to be right and wrong. There will be points at which their views will overlap, for example, in wanting to allow freedom for individuals as well as a pattern of authority in the state.

In Australia the different states – New South Wales, Victoria, Queensland, and so on – have their own parliaments making laws for each state. But in Canberra there is also a Federal Parliament legislating in those matters in which there is a common interest that crosses state boundaries. In a similar way, the ethics of Christians and non-Christians may come together. There are points at which their interests overlap, but it does not mean their ethics are the same. The source of their moral knowledge may be different, they may have different motives for behaving as they do, or they may have different goals. None of these things denies the common ground they may occupy.

An Ethic of People's Experiences

The story of the Church is not simply about matters that were settled in the past. It is not static but is a dynamic story which is continuing. Some of the questions the early Church asked about the Jesus way of life are no longer of interest to us. Most of us are not concerned with the problems of serving in a Roman army that acknowledged the emperor as divine but we are constantly finding new things about which we are concerned. Our experience and the pressures on us from the wider society invite us to reflect further on what we have until now assumed Christianity was all about. We have questions about world population and global economy, segregation and different patterns of living together, and so on. They pose new questions for the Christian community and require new answers.

The significance of this ongoing story for our ethics can be seen in the fact that it is only relatively recently that Western society turned its back on slavery. It is even more recent that women in Britain ceased to be treated as mere chattels. It is only in this century that they got the vote and their humanity began to be recognised as being equal to that of men. In the latter part of the century the Church has reflected on the role of women in its ministry, and amid much heart-searching and anguish the ministry of a number of churches has at least formally been opened to them, the most high-profile debate being within the Church of England.

The point is not made to raise questions about the rightness of such changes. It is to illustrate the way in which **human experience suggests that there is apparently always more to say about what it means to be an honest Christian community acting with integrity**. The story continues, and as it does so we appreciate more of what we believe is the right way forward for the people of God. We build on the wisdom we have received from the past as we constantly restate and understand, in new ways, the values of our community.

Notice, though, it is not a restatement that comes just from Church leaders or assemblies. The whole community is involved. It is tempting to think that as far as Christian ethics is concerned, those who will tell us what is right and wrong will be those with professional skills in interpreting the Bible, whether they be pastors, or teachers, or scholars. In particular we look to those who can, with some skill, get behind the text and tell us its significance for our times and the problems we have. Such people certainly have an important part to play in the way the Christian community takes its decisions, though even their work is normally evaluated by the remainder of the community of scholars.

Importantly, there is a place for the whole community in developing the story. **Everyone who is part of the Christian community brings their experiences to the community, and they matter**. Sometimes, when some of our community have views that we think are based on prejudice, one of the questions we rightly ask is, 'Have you ever met a person who is . . . ?' The hidden message is that experience affects the values we hold, because it invites us to match our views against reality. The result is that experience often makes us think again about the attitudes we adopt. Our attitudes about people of other races often change once we have got to know them. In the same way attitudes to cohabitation often change when one of our own family is involved. We begin to ask new questions and look deeper into what precisely is happening and what the real issues involved are. When we became aware of AIDS in the West, a commonly held assumption among Christians was that it was the result of a homosexual lifestyle that was sinful, and that determined attitudes towards those who were HIV positive. AIDS was seen in some circles as primarily a moral problem, rather than a medical one. It was as people began to meet those who were HIV positive from other causes, for example, being given infected blood, that moral attitudes began to change.

Yet for the story to develop we need more than our general experiences. There are those around us who are able to shed light on our morality through their specialist knowledge, and it is needed. The view that people of some races are less intelligent, and hence of less worth than others, is one that has been met by scientists. That is similar to the idea that used to be held that women were incapable of making the decisions that warranted giving them the vote. Economists help us understand what is really going on in world markets and that helps us make decisions about the morality of trading practices: what appears on the outside to be innocent trading often turns out to pose major moral difficulties when the experts have analysed those practices. The expertise of research scientists has revolutionised our understanding of what happens before birth, and influenced the views we take of abortion. It has also presented us with problems. For example, we now know that many fertilised eggs are rejected by women's bodies in the normal course of events. That leaves us wondering whether life begins with the fertilising of the egg or when the fertilised egg is implanted in the womb. Relief workers help us to see when the obvious acts of charity are not at all appropriate in a given situation and that the right action is – to those of us who do not understand the thinking of the recipients of our charity – apparently foolish.

To repeat, then, our moral standards are part of what it is to be a community. **In forming our standards and approach to ethics we draw on, and reflect, the story from the past and the ongoing story in the present**. Those with various professional skills and understanding have important roles, but the whole community has a part to play, simply because the whole community shapes its story. It may be difficult to bring together all the insights that are available, but bit by bit they do tend to come together, and opinions change as we appreciate the wisdom we receive from others in our particular community. The result is that as we become part of the community that owns that story, so we take upon ourselves those values which it proclaims and its story embodies.

Morality is just one of the aspects of life which people become aware of when they commit themselves to a community and begin to live according to the values which are learned as people become involved in the story, part of which means learning from those around us who teach and exemplify it. Sometimes the values are explicit, sometimes implicit as we pick up the nuances of what the community says and does and as we watch the way it applies those values to various aspects of life.

The Community's Role

This idea that ethics is always the ethics of a community has some implications for the way we use our moral beliefs. First, it is worth noticing that one effect is that **the community sets the boundaries of what is acceptable and what is unacceptable**. In the case of Christian ethics this is to be seen in the prohibitions that are obviously part of the ethic. As we will see, they represent the boundaries within which people live authentic lives in the community. They say what kind of things are outside the nature of the community.

Second, **the community has a role to play in checking the validity of what people may think are authentic moral claims**. Sometimes those claims are clear and explicit and it is relatively easy to understand what is being said and to decide whether it is in harmony with what is believed to be genuine Christian teaching. The situation ethics of Joseph Fletcher is one position which has caused serious discussion among Christians about whether it is an acceptable variant of the Christian faith. As such it has been subjected to scrutiny by many people in the community who, without any official status, are acting as guardians of Christian morality. That is right and correct, for if the ethic is derived from the community, then the community must consider what is a faithful representation of its position, and what is not. This is not to say that there are firm and established criteria which must be met, but as has already been suggested there are boundaries and the community polices what is claimed in its name, albeit usually in a very unofficial way.

Sometimes, though, the claims are rather more subtle. We have already seen that there is a tradition that says that the moral authority of the Bible is expressed in specific rules and in some cases we might want to agree. The response of many Christians to the question of the moral standing of homosexual practices is to say, 'See what the Bible has to say about it.' Scripture does say some things about this and it seems to give the answers that people often want. But its teaching can be far less obvious. If we ask about the moral standing of the way the media at times appear to intrude into the private lives of public figures who in some ways seem to invite media coverage, we have a problem, for about this the Bible says nothing. What are we to say, then? The answer that is often given is that where there is nothing explicit in the Bible we ought to use the principles which are to be found in the Bible. The problem with this is that, before we know it, we are the ones deciding what the relevant principles are. This is where the community has a large part to play, again because it is the check that a principle really is present and is as we are told.

Third, **at times the community nature of ethics means that there is more to be taken into account than simply the ethical issues**. The **beliefs** of the community play a part. An illustration of this is to be found in the problems that surround our understanding of divorce. The problems are not there because there are some lofty principles about marriage and human relationships, or the care of children. For the most part such principles do not attract debate. For Christians, however, there is an issue about the relative significance of what they ought to do and what they can do. Divorce raises the question of how far the morality of divorce is influenced by men and women who live such damaged lives that at times they are unable to make the relationships that successful marriage requires. To put the problem another way, the ethics of the Christian community is not an isolated phenomenon but draws on the beliefs that the community holds – in this case about the place of ideals in relation to what is possible.

Moral Absolutes

The common ground that exists between different communities is where we can look for those moral injunctions that are held to be true across communities. The search for moral absolutes –

the moral rules or principles that ought to apply to every human being irrespective of race or creed – is important, for the idea of such absolutes gives a sense of certainty and security in moral life. Absolutes mean there is more to the way we behave than personal preferences or the preferences of particular groups.

Each community is likely to have its own absolutes in the sense that there may be issues over which its members are not prepared to compromise, often because they are seen as intrinsic to the nature of the group. We have seen what those absolutes were for Joseph Fletcher and John Murray, both coming from the Christian community. One found an absolute in the overarching principle of love. The other found absolutes in the Ten Commandments. Clearly such absolutes may be held by other communities, though interpreted in different ways, so that many Christians may agree with Fletcher in seeing love as an absolute, yet not implement it in the way that Fletcher does.

The big question is whether there are absolutes that apply to all the communities and if there are, how we decide what they are. This will be part of our concern in the next chapter.

There are many problems with claims for the supremacy of a Christian morality, not least, knowing exactly what is being claimed, but such claims often reflect a failure to acknowledge that ethics comes from different communities which have different ways of life and different values. Such claims miss the point. Our ethics reflect our communities, with their own histories, values and models. If this argument is saying, 'We wish everyone else held the same views as us,' then fine. But if it means, 'We have the true ethic and it could be transposed in its entirety into their communities, even though they are not part of ours,' it is doubtful if it could be done without splitting the receiving group. As we will see, there is more to Christian ethics than a series of moral laws. Students in the swinging sixties who said that they could not see why they should accept Christian ideas of what was right and wrong because they did not believe in God, had got it right. They were not in the Christian community and accordingly did not accept its way of life.

6

Natural Law

One well-established way of approaching ethics is known as **natural law**, with the related ideas of natural justice and natural rights. We will be thinking mainly of natural law, but there are three significant features that all three of these related terms share:

- There are ways of behaving that apply to all human beings, irrespective of their backgrounds and upbringing. Natural law transcends national laws in its universal application.

- Natural law is known apart from any religious teaching, or divine revelation. It is accessible to human beings through reflection on their humanity.

- Natural law is an ethical idea that is common to Christians and non-Christians alike.

Theologically the idea of natural law raises the question of whether moral knowledge can be gained apart from Scripture, and among theologians this has been a matter of dispute. Traditionally the Roman Catholic Church has looked to natural law to decide how all human beings should live. Historically they have claimed that moral knowledge can be gained by using reason. Orthodox Christians have argued that it can be known by looking at human nature. Protestants have sometimes accepted forms of natural law, but often with reservations about its theological soundness. The idea that we can know what is right apart from revelation is hard for some to accept.

This idea that what is morally right and wrong can be known through reason has a long history, being accepted by both the Greeks and Romans. Plato argued that natural justice was done when human beings fulfilled their function in life, and had the role for which they were suited by temperament and training. Aristotle made a distinction between natural justice and conventional justice and argued that lawyers could argue beyond the laws of the community to laws of nature that are universally applicable. The Stoics held that the virtuous life is one in conformity with nature, and nature is basically rational. Cicero held that while the State had its laws to which rulers were answerable, the whole State was subject to the higher law of justice, which he described as the law of God.

Following the Maker's Instructions

From a Christian point of view natural law uses reason to look for moral statements that arise from human nature. At the heart of it is the belief that the world is the creation of God who gave human beings reason with which to reflect on human nature and discover how they ought to act. The result of this creation is that different natural entities are said to have their own nature and laws that govern them. Part of this reflection is that we can see that there are natural laws which are appropriate to the whole of humanity as part of creation, and which ought to be followed if we are to function in the ways in which we were intended to.

One way of looking at the significance of natural law is to make an analogy with, say, buying a lawnmower. With the mower we will probably get a booklet telling us how to treat it if we are to get the best from it. It requires cleaning and oiling, and should generally be used in certain ways. If we do not follow the instructions it will break, or at least be inefficient in cutting the grass. The manufacturer is telling us about the nature of the mower. He knows the materials he has used in its production and the treatment they will stand. He also knows the best way of using it to do the intended job.

This means that he knows what will damage the mower and prevent it from functioning as it should, and if we are wise we follow the instructions. These instructions reflect the nature of the machine.

If we apply the analogy to human beings, the argument goes that we too have instructions for living in the way human beings were meant to live. Some Christians would claim that these are given in the Bible, which in this context functions as a kind of handbook. Other people, Christians and non-Christians, might claim that while we may have some instructions set out as in a manufacturer's handbook, we find out from experience what are the things that make us human. So each generation discovers, with the aid of what has gone before, what is 'natural' for human beings. In the Roman Catholic tradition this has taken the form of a belief that the human person has a function and that the various organs also have their functions, which together make for the good of the whole person. If we establish what those functions are, then we can see what is morally right and wrong.

Examples of the way this idea of natural law is applied are easy to find. Roman Catholic teaching on artificial contraception is a good example. The claim is that sexual organs were made for purposes of reproduction. That is their nature and their correct use. Hence artificial contraception prevents a natural function and is wrong. Although this form of natural law argument is usually associated with the Roman Catholic Church, there are times when it is used by Protestants as well. An example is the way in which the idea of natural use is applied to homosexual practices in two ways. First, the human body is not physically adapted for anal sex, so it cannot be claimed that is its function. Because they are not in accord with the nature of being human, it is said to follow that such acts are 'unnatural' and morally wrong. Second, if it is true that the function of the human reproductive system is to produce children, as homosexual sex acts cannot do that, then such acts are also morally wrong.

However attractive the argument might be, there is something flawed about it. First, **to limit human beings to biological functions is both selective and at variance with the nature of human beings**. We are rational beings and capable of thought about our physical activities. We also have emotions and hopes and have psychological needs. This is not to pass any judgment on artificial contraception or on homosexual sex, but it is to say that when we start to appeal to the maker's instructions on how we ought to function, we need to recognise the danger of using only one aspect of what makes us human.

Second, **how do we know what physical organs were primarily made for?** It may seem obvious that reproduction is the true function of the sex organs, but how do we know it is so? We could describe their function in other ways, for example, that they are for producing personal pleasure. Unless we can say more about the claim, it is like saying that right arms were made for lifting pints of ale to our mouths, and that is a claim few of us would want to support when we are serious! Bodily organs can serve more than one function.

Third, **the claim is really about the laws of nature, rather than about obligatory laws**. There is a difference between them. When we think about laws many of us think about the legislation that comes from Parliament or our local council offices, whether it be, 'Stop at red traffic lights', 'Do not walk on the grass', 'Buy a ticket before you board the train', or 'Marriages must be witnessed'.

They tell us what to do. But there are also laws of nature that are descriptive. They tell us such things as the temperature at which water boils, and that what goes up must, left to itself, come down. Statements about human nature are generally of this second kind. To say that this or that part of the body is designed for particular functions is not, in itself, saying that it is therefore wrong to use it for another purpose. That is a further question. We may want to say that if we want to get the best out of our mower we ought to do certain things, but this is not to say that we must do them.

Fourth, **the claim that we ought to live in accordance with our nature tends to carry with it the assumption that our**

nature is constant, and this is very much open to question. We are beings who live in history and are affected by the world and times in which we live, and that includes the prejudices and assumptions that we make. From time to time it is possible to hear the claim that a woman's place is in the home, or that such and such is 'woman's work'. Yet experience tells us that what we have taken to be 'woman's work' can be done by men. It would be naive to think that everything is interchangeable – men cannot give birth, for example – but more and more of the boundaries between male and female are being removed as the two genders share what was traditionally thought to be natural to one of them. The point is that a case can be made for saying that, in this sense, human nature is constantly developing. Christians make a case for this development by saying that at the resurrection Christ ushered in a new creation with human nature transformed by grace.

A modern account of natural law from a Christian standpoint is to be found in Sheila Upjohn's book *Why Julian Now?* She quotes a telling passage from Dorothy L. Sayers' *The Mind of the Maker:*

> There is a universal moral *law*, as distinct from a moral *code*, which consists in certain statements of fact about the nature of man; and by behaving in conformity with which, man enjoys his true freedom . . . The more closely the moral code agrees with the natural law, the more it makes for freedom in human behaviour; the more widely it departs from the natural law, the more it tends to enslave mankind and to produce catastrophes called 'judgements of God' . . .
>
> Regulations about doing no murder and refraining from theft and adultery belong to the moral code and are based on certain opinions held by Christians in common about the value of human personality. Such 'laws' as these are not statements of fact, but rules of behaviour. Societies which do not share Christian opinion about human values are logically

quite justified in repudiating the code based on that opinion.

If however, Christian opinion turns out to be right about the facts of human nature, then the dissenting societies are exposing themselves to that judgement of catastrophe which awaits those who defy the natural law.

Sheila Upjohn makes the point in this way:

The secular society has, logically, repudiated the code based on Christian opinion about the facts of human nature. There is surely a case for suspecting that, as a result, that society, where angry motorists kill each other, schools have to be protected by security fences, ninety-year-olds are robbed and raped, where patients attack their doctors and children their teachers, and where it is no longer safe to leave a toddler unattended for fear he will be abducted and murdered by other children – may be facing a 'judgement of catastrophe'. And if it is, it will not be because, in some simplistic way, God is angry with us, but because we have left something out right at the beginning of our calculation about human nature, which throws out the whole of the rest of the sum.

The point both Sheila Upjohn and Dorothy L. Sayers make is that we digress from that natural law in which we are meant to live in harmony. The result is that, although we may live within the legal constraints of our society, we may not necessarily be living in accordance with our natural self.

The feature of this line of thought that is significant for our present purposes is that there is nothing in the appeal to human nature, as we have been using it here, that makes it in any way Christian – it is an argument that is common to all human beings.

Reasoning for the Common Good

There is another view of natural law that comes from reflection on fundamental human nature. This view claims that it is a law that knows no boundaries between human beings, for its very character makes it accessible to all.

H.L.A. Hart illustrated what this might mean by taking the premise that the basis of human action is survival. That is certainly a reasonable assumption when we reflect on our own and others' experience: we want to survive, and people sometimes sue hospitals and people such as doctors and road users if they do things that put survival at risk.

This premise of survival can give rise to further reflection, from which we may get a number of moral precepts, such as the following:

- There ought to be a restriction of violence which results in killing and harm. Such violence is an obvious threat to our survival.

- There ought to be mutual tolerance and compromise. This is a more positive way of promoting survival.

- There must be a measure of human love.

- Because there are limited resources we must respect property. In other words, we need to protect those things that help us to survive.

The mediaeval scholar, Thomas Aquinas, who has had a great influence on Roman Catholic ethical thinking, taught that reflection will show us the mind of God discernible through human nature. By this means we can discern some first principles that will promote good. In particular Aquinas thought we could discern those ends towards which we tend by nature. They are ends we share with all living substances, for example, the desire to survive. They are also ends we share with other animals, and these will include the desire to procreate and educate our young. Then there are those ends appropriate to us as human beings, for example, that we ought to act according to reason and live in society with one another. A moment's reflection will show us how universal human rights can be derived from such an analysis. They include the rights to life, education, freedom of speech and opinion.

These first principles are binding on us. On occasions, however, we draw implications from such first principles that further reflection tells us are invalid and false. The result is that because the implied claims are not necessarily correct and binding, we need to treat them with caution. Natural law in Aquinas's account is limited in application but provides a basis for moral thought and life.

John Locke, the seventeenth-century philosopher, argued for natural rights, although these are not about an individual's self-interest. He claimed that by rational reflection we come to discover certain fixed and permanent moral truths. Thus he claimed that we find we all have a right to life, liberty and property and have a moral responsibility for one another to ensure these rights.

Aquinas believed that civil law rested on natural law and it is not hard to understand why. We can make out a case, for example, that murder is a crime against natural law and that natural justice requires that evil people are answerable for what they do. It has been suggested that the Nuremberg trials at the end of the Second World War were trying crimes against humanity and as such were invoking natural justice. The same charge of crimes against humanity is made against instigators of atrocities in Bosnia in the 1990s. These are charges based on an assumption of natural law in that we do not need to be told what revelation has to say about such things. Across cultures and State boundaries there has been a common recognition that the human race has been diminished by what happened. Reflection has shown the enormity of what was done. Another example is the way in which Martin Luther King invoked natural law in his 'Letter from a Birmingham Jail' as a way of justifying civil disobedience.

In contrast to such uses of natural law is civil law. It

specifies what natural law does not tell us, for example, laws about parking regulations and wheel clamping. Civil law obviously is also about those things that are in the public interest and hence may reflect moral interests.

Again there is nothing intrinsic to this view of natural law that requires a religious faith or religious precepts. It is a moral law that is open to all and as such is sometimes held to be a common meeting point for human beings of different faiths and ideologies, and those of none.

Before we end this chapter it is worth noting that the standing of natural law in ethics is not settled. The problems concern the way we ought to view ourselves and hence what sort of moral statements we can legitimately make on the basis of human nature. It means that in recent decades there have been various attempts to rethink the role it has in ethics, and there have been various attempts to restate it. What is unchanging is the belief that it is possible to look beyond human laws to a law that is held to be common to us all. Such a law goes beyond the codes of behaviour set by State legislators and beyond the moral codes of different religions. It is this belief and the search for an adequate expression of this law that unites Christian and non-Christian in a common task and gives a meeting ground in ethics.

We have now considered three aspects of ethics which are shared by Christian and non-Christian systems:

- They have a common content.

- They are rooted in their communities.

- They use the idea of natural law.

There are also common concerns, one of which is justice, which we will look at in the next chapter.

7

A Concern for Justice

In the previous three chapters we looked at the way in which Christian ethics is, in general, similar to other forms of ethics in its content, community roots and in its use of the idea of natural law. It is not simply in its nature that there are similarities, though. Christian ethics shares some of the concerns of the wider community for the world in which we live. For example, there is a shared concern about the environment and about human freedom. In this chapter we will consider the shared concern for and understanding of justice, in part because it is an example of these shared concerns and also because justice is important in society generally. But there is a further reason why justice has been chosen as an example of shared concerns, and that is the important part it plays in Christian ethics.

It is tempting to think that Christian ethics only affects me and the world around me. After all, the most immediate, and often the most pressing, ethical problems we face are personal. If I get the wrong change ought I to tell the girl on the checkout? What ought I to think about my brother cohabiting with his girlfriend? And so on. There is a wider range of less personal issues for Christians, though. For example, how ought I to react if my coffee is cheap because workers in the field are poorly paid? Ought the prosperous nations of the world to flourish at the expense of the poor? These are questions of the morality of people living together in a world where what we do in one part of the world impinges on what happens in another. They are questions of social morality, and typically involve matters of justice.

Matters of justice have a difficult time in some branches of the Church, where it is seen as an optional extra to be considered if there are time and resources available from mission. And of course if we start with that idea there never are enough time and resources available! But the Bible has a lot to say about justice, which is clearly important in God's eyes and should be important for his people too. Typically Jeremiah 23:5 says '. . . I will raise up to David a righteous Branch, a King who will reign wisely and do what is just and right in the land.' And the Psalmist: 'I know that the Lord secures justice for the poor' (Psalm 140:12). There are repeated appeals for justice in the Old Testament, particularly in the prophets Amos and Micah. They were especially concerned for the poor and vulnerable in society, a theme taken up eight centuries later by Jesus. For the prophets worship, festivals and rites were without meaning unless they were accompanied by the pursuit of justice, 'Away with the noise of your songs! I will not listen to the music of your harps. But let justice roll on like a river, righteousness like a never-failing stream' (Amos 5:23–4). The two – religious ceremony and justice – ought to go together. 'He has showed you, O man, what is good. And what does the Lord require of you? To act justly and to love mercy and to walk humbly with your God' (Micah 6:8).

Justice, then, has been an important concern for God's people in the past and it is an integral part of Christian morality today.

What is Justice?

Over the years there have been a variety of attempts to say what justice is. For example:

- Justice is about making sure that everyone has the role in society for which they are suited. It is unjust to consign a Nobel Prize scientist to a permanent job of washing the dishes. Similarly, it is unjust to make a bad organiser and poor leader run a large company where they are overwhelmed.

- Justice is promoting a society which defends the rights of all and gives everyone an equal chance in life.

- A society is just when there is the greatest happiness that it is possible to produce.

The problem of finding a satisfactory account can be illustrated by thinking about life in a certain school. Mrs Johnson teaches young children. She likes to give time to them as individuals because they each have their own particular needs and she wants them to succeed. Each week she tries to give each one of them the same amount of time and attention. Indeed, she has a timetable so that during each week she will see each child for a certain amount of time irrespective of who they are, and she is meticulous in keeping to her plan. She is efficient and effective, though the parents of one of the slower children are certain that there is a gap opening between their child and some of the more able children, even though they all get equal time. Sometimes over coffee Mrs Johnson talks to her colleagues about this way of organising things and commends it to them as being fair for everyone. No one gets more than anyone else in her classroom.

Mrs Lyons, who teaches in the next room, listens and compares it with her own pattern of work. She also helps individuals, but gives more attention to the less able than to the able. As she listens to Mrs Johnson she gets quite anxious about what she is doing and wonders if giving more time to some than to others is fair to all her children. Perhaps Mrs Johnson has a fairer system by giving an equal amount of her time to each child?

What is fair in a classroom with so many different children at different stages? What does the word mean? We may say that of course Mrs Johnson is fair. But then other questions arise. Is she respecting them as individuals with their own needs? Is that desirable?

There is a tradition among some Christians that justice means something like 'getting what you deserve'. By that we often mean that because someone has done something of which we disapprove, it is right that they suffer some unpleasantness. That is what is due to them. We may even assume this is what justice means with God. We have done evil things so it is only right that God should seek retribution. Hence we all deserve to be punished and justice will be done when that punishment is carried out.

There is no doubt that justice can appear hard: 'You got what you deserved.' That is a rather negative view of justice, though. More positively, in everyday life there is another sense of justice which we use when we talk about fairness. It is not about Mrs Johnson's equal distribution of resources, but about fairness for the disadvantaged and those who are treated badly. It is the point of view that Mrs Lyons takes as she gives more time to the less able. The prophet Isaiah had this view in mind when he wrote of God telling the people, 'I, the Lord, love justice; I hate robbery and iniquity' (Isaiah 61:8).

Justice and Responsibility. Justice is more than simply helping the disadvantaged, though. It is also about acknowledging that people should be able to take responsibility for their lives. It is not unusual for some parents to try and prevent or delay their children becoming independent of them. Others indulge their children so much that they do not learn that to live in a society means respecting others' needs, if we expect them to respect ours. Other parents are overprotective.

These ways of treating children raise questions about how just such practices are. We recognise the need for care and protection for small children, but when it is overdone with older children we usually believe that such parents are not being fair to their children. The reason is that the opportunity to learn to take responsibility for their lives is being denied them. We sometimes realise this in the way we handle children.

Experienced teachers sometimes think they have spotted troublemakers in a new class before anything wrong has been done. They notice the way other children look at disrupters and the general air of expectancy the latter arouse. Or they notice the look on their faces and years of experience tell them there is trouble ahead. It would be possible to inflict something nasty on such children *before* they offend, on the principle of getting in first and deterring anyone with thoughts of misbehaving. It may be an understandable thing to do, but it certainly raises questions about the justice of it. The reason is that it does not respect the child as a responsible being. If he does something wrong we may say it is just that he is punished, but to 'punish' before it happens is to deny the child the opportunity to be responsible for his actions, and we would probably say that is unjust.

We usually accept as a general rule that it is just to let human beings take responsibility for their lives. This is why aid agencies tend to encourage self-help programmes rather than handouts for the poor, a very Christian idea of justice too, as we will see when we have thought further about the matter.

Justice as Fair Distribution. Mrs Johnson gave her pupils equal treatment: no one got more than anyone else. Mrs Lyons acted differently, so was she being unjust?

To help us look further at the two teachers, let us take the case of Stella, who is a black girl working in a go-ahead company. She is talented and intelligent, efficient at her job, personable and popular with her colleagues. Moreover, she is helpful towards the general public. In fact, she is a real asset to the firm in every way. But over a period of time some of her friends at work became concerned for her. There were less able girls with less experience being promoted over her, while Stella's job prospects became more and more remote. One of her friends asked her why she thought this was, and the only explanation she could think of was that it was the colour of her skin. Her friend's reply was, 'What has that to do with it?'

What indeed had the colour of her skin to do with the job

she was doing? But it seemed to count against her promotion. There was an injustice here.

In the same way we would no doubt say that it is unfair if all women with painted fingernails could go to the head of the queue at supermarket checkouts. What have their fingernails to do with it? Or perhaps all ginger-headed men should be served first in pubs. Hair colour does not seem relevant and so we would again say that there would be an injustice in such an instance.

We can express this by saying that **we should treat everyone in the same way as long as there are no relevant grounds for making distinctions between them**. For example, when Kevin, who is a boy in a wheelchair, is taken to the front of the crowd to get an uninterrupted view of the Queen passing in her coach, we usually recognise that there is a good reason for it. It is not only that we feel some sympathy for him, but much more we accept that being confined to a wheelchair is a relevant reason for him to have special treatment in that situation. If it were a matter of selecting books in a library, however, we would not feel that being in a wheelchair was sufficient reason for Kevin to have first choice of the new books. The wheelchair is irrelevant in that case.

We would, though, think it unjust if Kevin were automatically taken to the front of the crowd and other boys in wheelchairs were left at the back of the crowd where they could not see. In so far as they are the same as Kevin, it would be just for them to be treated in the same way. After all, if there is sufficient space, why should they not receive equal treatment?

The principle, then, is that **where there are relevant differences people should be treated differently. Where there are no relevant differences they should be treated the same**. To put it briefly, justice means we treat equals equally (for example, everyone like Kevin) and treat unequals unequally (Kevin in relation to those not in wheelchairs). This is appealing to what is known as **distributive justice**.

This is the principle we can see at work in the eighth century

BC when there was a lot of wealth in Israel, but in the hands of a small percentage of the population. There was a lot of injustice in the way that wealth was used and the prophet Amos spoke out against the social evils of the time (see Amos chapters 2 and 5). Landsharks were taking advantage of the poor by making loans to them that could not be repaid and then seizing their land as payment for the debt. Some men were so poor they were selling themselves into slavery in order to get the money to meet their obligations. The courts were corrupt: the system meant to protect the disadvantaged was being abused by those able to bribe the judges, and the powerless poor were losing their cases simply because they were poor. In chapter 8 of the book Amos speaks of the way in which scales were fixed to the disadvantage of the poor. It was because of what he saw that he and the other faithful prophets of the time called for justice. The book asks, 'Why should the rich take advantage of the poor?' They may have been the most disadvantaged in a prosperous land, but that was not a sufficient reason for the treatment they received. 'Is poverty a sufficient reason for them to be denied justice in the courts?' 'Is it a good reason for scales to be fixed to their disadvantage?' Amos' response is a loud 'NO!' It is a scream for justice, 'Hate evil, love good, and establish justice in the gate' (Amos 5:15). In other words, treat people equally unless there are relevant differences between them.

This plea for justice has enormous implications for the morality of our social lives, not least for the way Mrs Johnson and Mrs Lyons organise their teaching. If the differences between Mrs Lyons' children are genuinely significant, then in the interests of justice she should treat them differently. Mrs Johnson, on the other hand, may be doing a disservice to those children who are relevantly different from the remainder of the class by treating them the same. The teachers would have to judge whether there are any differences relevant to the use of their resources.

There are plenty of cases where it is appropriate to ask if justice is being done:

- We need to look at the lives of single parents to see what marks them out for special treatment.

- Ought we to treat all our own children the same?

- Is a person's gender or sexual orientation significant in deciding who should be office-bearers in the church?

- Ought there to be positive discrimination in favour of deprived areas?

- Ought the rich nations to cancel the debts of the poor?

These may not be easy issues to resolve, because we may find reasons which appear to cut across what would otherwise be just actions – for example, in the case of women's ordination there are theological considerations to take into account. But this does not absolve us from the responsibility of seriously examining these issues in the context of justice. To do what justice demands may not be popular, but it is one of the major principles in Christian ethics and ought to be taken seriously.

Justice and Love

If, as Jesus said, Christian morality can be expressed in terms of love, then where does justice fit? It is a matter of debate, but it is not hard to see a relationship. Love is a notoriously difficult principle to apply, not least because our love is likely to reduce into sentimentality. Justice helps to anchor love and give it direction. On the other hand, appeals to justice can be harsh and legalistic and devoid of love. Those in positions of authority need love, which adds a human dimension to an abstract application of rules. The two principles need each other as checks and balances.

We can with some justification claim that justice is simply one aspect of love in that it is loving to see that those who are being disadvantaged are protected from oppression and exploitation. Love demands that they need the protection of a just system of dealing with one another if human worth is to be recognised.

Justice is not solely the concern of Christians. The need for justice is recognised by men and women of goodwill who start from a variety of assumptions. We have seen the way in which it is reflected in the Christian Scriptures, however, and the importance it has in biblical thought. Biblically the key idea is not that of just deserts, but of a fair distribution of goods. This issues in social concerns and a desire to respond to human need.

8

Tools for the Job

We have been considering some of the aspects of Christian ethics that are shared with other forms of ethics. It has a similar content, is similarly rooted in its community and appeals to natural law. It also has something in common with the ethical concerns of other groups, and we considered justice as an example.

There comes a time when ethical theories have to be translated into the harsh reality of making decisions, so having decided what we believe is the appropriate way of deciding right from wrong, we have to look at specific situations and apply our theories. Christians are like non-Christians in that they rely on various 'tools' of decision making to help them. In particular, Christians often look for help from the Bible, but in practice they also use other aids. In this chapter we will look at the way in which four such aids are of help, all of which are used by non-Christians as well as by Christians. Here too there are aspects of Christian ethics that are similar to those of other groups.

A Good Conscience

There is nothing about conscience that is only applicable in Christian ethics. On the contrary, it is an idea that is very familiar to us whether we have a religious allegiance or not. It can have a powerful influence on us because it is characteristic of our conscience that it operates when something wrong is done or contemplated. Then we can justifiably talk of having a troubled conscience. At those times when we are doing what is right, our consciences keep quiet and do not trouble us.

A general description of a troubled conscience would be what happens when **people come up against themselves and face demands from within themselves**. The helpful thing about this description is that it presents the conscience as operating in a contest: me and my conscience. This is why people rightly say 'my conscience won't let me . . .' and we understand what the speaker means. This idea of a contest, then, is a helpful starting point when we attempt to say what the features of conscience are:

- It is one of the sides in a contest, accusing the other of a wrong deed or thought.

- It acts as a witness that an action – past, present or future – is good or bad.

- It is not a judge that pronounces a verdict – it is *our* choice whether we take any notice of our conscience.

At various times people have assumed that because our conscience tells us what is right and wrong, then it is the voice of God speaking to us. If it is the voice of God we would expect our conscience always to be correct in what it tells us, but unfortunately it is not that simple. Our conscience can be educated and trained. What is acceptable to people's consciences in one culture is not necessarily so in another. Experience tells us that if we do something wrong for long enough, we can deaden our conscience so that it ceases to trouble us. The contrary is also true. We can repeatedly tell ourselves that such-and-such an action is wrong, and after a time our conscience reacts accordingly, even if everyone else agrees that the action is right. The truth is that our consciences are not automatically programmed to whatever is morally right and wrong and we can, and sometimes do, manipulate them and hence they may give us the wrong messages.

We can easily understand why this is so:

- Our conscience does not know how to make moral judgments. That is what we do apart from our consciences which then express the judgments we make.

- Conscience does not have immediate access to the information we need to make some of our judgments – we have to feed it.

- We sometimes find that what we thought was conscience was actually our prejudice and self-interest.

None of this means that we should not take any notice of what our conscience tells us. Far from it. But we need to realise that while it is a very helpful tool in making moral judgments, it is not infallible. It is like a signpost in a film comedy. It seems to guide us in the right direction, but someone may have turned the post round.

With the possibility of our conscience being misguided it would be foolish to treat it as the objective voice of God. It will follow what we take to be the principles for acting in a morally correct way, and needs to be trained.

The conscience's role in religious life was described by Martin Luther who made a distinction between conscience prior to faith and after faith. Prior to faith he thought it did not tell us what we should do, but defended us against God's demands. In other words, it recognises what we can do and assures us that we are doing our best. After a person begins to follow Christ, Luther believed that conscience takes God's side and acts against what a person previously believed. It tells us that what we do is not good enough.

Despite its changeable nature, though, it has an important role in moral life. **It pulls us up sharply when we are**

tempted to do something that we would otherwise not do. It is like a smoke alarm that warns us that something *may* be wrong. A man who is invited to join a group in planning a retirement celebration for a colleague may be tempted to think that the idea of a *This Is Your Life* evening is a great idea. He may even think it would be fun to include people from the past who would embarrass his colleague. But then his conscience may trouble him. It may indeed be all right to go ahead with what is proposed, but his conscience acts as an alarm inviting him to look a little more closely at what is proposed.

In the seventeenth century Jeremy Taylor gave some guidelines for deciding whether or not we should follow our consciences. The following list is based on what he had to say:

- Suspect the conscience when we are not prepared to look at details, that is to say, when we are happy to accept general ideas, rather than looking at the awkward questions that may be appropriate.

- Suspect the conscience when we only look at outcomes that confirm our views.

- Use reason as well as emotion.

- Know the principles we wish to follow.

- Even though they may be a minority follow reputable guides:
    1. 'Wise guides of the soul'.
    2. Those who know about the issue.
    3. Those whose office or job it is to deal with such things.
    4. Those who are impartial.

- Take actions at face value.

Our conscience is important in making decisions, but we need to be careful to bear in mind that it has to be seen as a reminder, rather than as a final standard.

Using Tradition

Tradition can play a big part in the life of the Church, though we may not like to admit it. After all, in the eyes of some, to say that we are traditional suggests we are in a rut and unwilling to change. Yet to be part of a church is to be part of a tradition. It may not have existed long, but each church group has its traditions. Roman Catholics have traditions that may not be the same as those of House Churches, or Baptists, or Methodists, or Anglicans, but they all have traditions in the way in which they worship and do things. Traditions reflect roots and history. They say things about being in a succession.

Tradition can help unite a group and give a sense of identity, and that is positive. It also has a role in moral life, for it enables us to look back on the wisdom of those who have been part of our community in the past and to learn from them. Following the group tradition is a way of preserving what has been good in the past.

There are dangers in tradition, though, and there are three that are worth noting. First, there is the danger that **tradition can be a hindrance rather than a help**, and this is true about tradition as a guide to what we take to be right and wrong. A church may teach that divorce is admissible in certain circumstances, but in practice the tradition is that its members do not divorce. That may have disastrous effects for a churchmember who, by the teaching of that church has good reasons for divorcing a partner. The life of the churchmember and that of the partner can be marred as a result. Another example is the denominations which in principle accept women ministers and priests, but still hold to the tradition that Church leadership should be invested in men. The resulting message is confused and hinders women going forward for ordination.

Tradition can hinder our relationship with God. Jesus recognised this when he had to deal with the Pharisees. On one occasion they asked Jesus why his disciples were eating food without first giving their hands a ceremonial washing, as was the tradition. Jesus's answer was to quote Isaiah, 'These people honour me with their lips, but their hearts are far from me. They worship me in vain; their teachings are but rules taught by men.' Then he said, 'You have let go of the commands of God and are holding on to the traditions of men' (Mark 7:1–8). Tradition got in the way of priorities.

Second, there is a danger that **tradition may hold us to what is now outdated and unnecessary**. The Jews in the early Church wanted to keep the Jewish tradition of requiring Gentiles to be circumcised when they joined God's people. As far as Paul (with his missionary experience of Gentile Christians) was concerned, the tradition was inappropriate when it came to Gentiles joining the Christian community. But for a time the argument continued, as tradition had to be faced and challenged for what it was in this case: an irrelevancy.

Third, **tradition can take an authority which becomes rigid**. It was so with the Pharisees and is so in some churches, for we take up entrenched positions over a host of things. To avoid innovations in worship we become over-insistent on preserving what has been done in the past. Similarly, because we are rigid in what we believe, we can fail to recognise that there are arguments over some ethical issues. Often rigidity means that we do not listen to what is being said about the matter under discussion because we do not want our position to be disturbed. One example is the way in which some Christians reacted to the Report of the Church of England Board of Social Responsibility, *Something To Celebrate*. At one point the Report said that to talk of 'living in sin' was pastorally unhelpful. Some of the instant reactions in the media were to denounce what the report had to say as being too liberal and condoning cohabitation. Irrespective of the rights and wrongs of the assertion, some of the reactions came from a tradition that had become so rigid that it was hard to hear what the Report was saying. In this case the Report was not saying that cohabitation was morally acceptable, but that the language we traditionally use to describe it is not always helpful. The traditional language had become frozen to the point where some were unable to disentangle language from practice.

There is a similar rigidity in the way in which some approach the debate about abortion. Some groups are only interested in the question of when the unborn gains moral standing, and this has become the traditional question for them to ask. Their position on this is so rigid that they do not hear the cry from a woman to choose whether to abort what is in her womb. Another area where some would claim that tradition is holding back the moral debate is that of homosexual practices. There is a traditional understanding of the biblical passages that seem relevant to this debate, which can be so rigid that alternative interpretations are not thought to be significant. This is not to say that alternative views are necessarily correct, but that the debate is hindered and relevant questions are not asked because of a rigid tradition.

It is worth remembering the obvious, namely, that traditions do change. For a long time the tradition of the Church of England was that ordination was only open to men. Yet the tradition has changed. Interestingly, this is not solely because the Church reviewed its doctrine of ordination. In a large part it was because the wider society began to listen to the arguments of those who said that there are injustices and anomalies in the way women are treated in society. This was the context in which the Church began to ask questions about its theology and understanding of Scripture. Changing tradition, whether in Church or State institutions, is often dependent upon a general feeling that current practice needs changing to meet new needs and ideas.

We need to bear in mind that in our traditional positions on ethical issues,

- we need to be open to the traditions needing restating,

- our traditional views need to be under regular review,

- traditions can and do change.

If the Church in previous centuries were like the Church in our times, it is likely that people did not really think that its views on slavery ought to be changed. Did some members of the Church ever think that their traditional views would change? Probably not.

Yet traditions matter, even though they may be a hindrance:

- They give us a means of checking new ideas against the accumulated wisdom of the past. The Children of God cult allegedly encouraged some of their women to engage in prostitution in order to encourage men to join their organisation. Our tradition is but one tool we have in putting such behaviour into perspective.

- Traditions enable us to join with Christians from other generations and places in a common understanding of the significance of some of the practices around us.

- It is a failing of each generation to imagine that previous generations were not as wise, or shrewd, or discerning as our own. Maybe they were not. But they have left us a heritage of experience and thought that helps us to manage change in our own times.

Thinking about the Consequences

At the beginning of the book we met the ideas of Mrs Thompson and Miss Argyle who both believed that the consequences of an action established whether it was morally acceptable or not. Christians generally believe that such a view does not do justice to the role of rules in Christian ethics. Nevertheless, there is a place for looking seriously at the likely outcome of our actions when we come to making decisions. It is easy to find illustrations of this. With an increasing concern for human rights, governments are now under pressure not to sell arms to foreign States unless there is some confidence that they will not be used to harass minority groups in those countries. In other words, the consequences of arms sales is of some importance.

Thinking about the consequences of what we do has a precedent in the New Testament. As we noted when thinking about John Murray's book *Principles of Conduct*, in his letter to the Corinthians, Paul showed that he was aware that there were those who thought that eating meat which had been offered to idols had religious significance. Paul thought it was a false idea, but in order that those with such ideas should not have their faith destroyed, his conclusion was, 'Therefore if what I eat causes my brother to fall into sin, I will never eat meat again, so that I will not cause him to fall' (1 Corinthians 8:13). Again, the consequences of his actions were important.

The likely outcomes are not always easy to predict, but this does not excuse us from doing the best we can to predict them. We may get them wrong, but that is the nature of taking decisions and is something we have to live with. Christian responsibility for other people requires that we do the best we can with the information we have available. Living a moral life can be very risky!

Knowledge of the Situation

It may seem strange to think that knowledge of the facts of a situation is relevant to the decisions we make about right and wrong, but it is. After all, it might be thought that right is right and wrong is wrong whatever the facts of the case. Yet we need to have relevant information before we make moral judgments. For example, in Britain a small boy named James Bulger was murdered by two older boys. It was a terrible incident, but part of the defence was that the two boys were influenced by watching a video. Knowledge of the way in which videos can affect the behaviour of young children was very relevant to the case, because without it there was only impression and hearsay on which to decide whether they were responsible for their crime.

It is not unusual for certain types of video and drugs to be blamed for a number of problems in society, and it is important that we have relevant and reliable information about their effects. One of the arguments that is sometimes used to ban pornography from shops is the effect it can have on those who use it. There may be more to coming to decisions than simply the consequences of pornography being available in shops, but this argument relies on a claim for which we need evidence.

Knowledge relevant to a situation can be a great help to us in coming to our decisions. But we need to be careful how it is interpreted. By itself knowledge of a series of facts does not give us moral direction. Facts need moral questions asked about them, for they do not, by themselves, provide moral answers. For example, because it is accepted practice in a particular firm that all the sales representatives claim reimbursement for more than they spend, it does not follow that the practice is right. It is tempting to think that because a certain state of affairs exists and is accepted, then it must be right, but the moral issues still remain, no matter how widespread a practice is.

We have thought about four factors which Christian ethics share with many non-Christian approaches to ethics in coming to decisions:

- People take notice of their consciences.

- They are influenced by the traditions of their communities.

- They note the likely consequences of what others do.

- They need any relevant knowledge.

It may be a surprise to some Christians, upon reflection,

to realise how much their own form of ethics can have in common with other positions.

However, there are some other features of Christian ethics which are either very different in defining the nature of Christian ethics, or different in the way in which common factors are interpreted and applied. Having recognised the points of similarity we are now ready to look at the more distinctive elements in Christian ethics.

9

What is Christian about Christian Ethics?

Christian ethics is a distinctive way of looking at how people behave. In earlier chapters of this book we have thought about the way in which this ethic relates to other aspects of ethics and the way in which it shares various features with non-Christian ethics. Whether Christians decide that an appeal to either rules or consequences best fits their understanding of Christianity, neither of them is the heart of Christian ethics and it is not by looking at Mr Jones and his friends that we can identify what is Christian about Christian ethics. There are other features that are distinctive.

In the remainder of the book we will be looking at four ways in which the distinctive nature of Christian ethics can be seen. Compared with the ethical positions we met in the story of the League of Family Values,

- it has a different starting place,
- it seeks different things,
- it makes its decisions on different grounds,
- it has a different source of moral knowledge.

Initially we will look at one of its theological starting places.

A God-based Ethic

Christian ethics is a theological ethic. That is to say, it is derived from God. That may seem obvious, for there are plenty of instances in Christian literature where there are moral commands which are attributed to God. But that is not the sense in which we claim that the ethic is derived from God. Rather, the moral standards of the Christian community are derived not from what God says, but from the kind of person he is. This has some implications for Christian ethics. It means that the basis of such an ethic is not to be found in the pragmatic search for a code of behaviour that will enable a society to run with the minimum of friction. Though a Christian ethic may have that effect, it is not the basis for it. Nor does it mean that ethics is, in its basic premises, changeable. If it is to be relevant across the ages we would expect there to be some elements of change in the way its basic teachings are able to be applied to changing situations, but at its core it is no more open to change than the nature of God can change. Our ideas of God are important in Christian ethics.

God as our Judge. Some people hold the view that God is an awesome, all-powerful being who is to be obeyed if we are not to face dreadful calamities. They see him as a vengeful God from whom we must expect punishment if we do not obey what he says. Often that punishment is thought to occur in this life and, when they have done things that they believe are very wrong, some people then wait for the punishment they think will follow. Maybe it will be a personal disaster, like being made redundant, or a member of the family having a serious illness, the severity of which is expected to match the misdemeanour. If it is not a punishment to be faced in this life it will be met in the next when the great judge opens his books and settles his accounts.

That kind of thinking has a long history. The children of Israel looked at the calamities they faced and decided that if only they were more obedient to God then they would have a far less troubled time. At one time the early disciples of Jesus held such a view. They came across a man who was blind from birth and asked Jesus whether it was because the man had sinned or his parents had sinned. Jesus's response was to say that it was neither, but rather it had happened so that 'the work of God might be displayed in his life' (John 9:1–7). It has its counterpart in some parts of the Church today where people think that if there is some serious difficulty in life about which we could have done nothing, for example, financial problems for which we are not responsible, or illness, then there must be a corresponding sin for which our misfortune is a punishment.

That is one view of God and it results in a particular view of ethics. Morality becomes a matter of appeasing God and this has implications for the way in which some people behave. Because of what are thought to be the consequences of moral failure it is likely to lead to a scrupulous attention to the detail of one's personal life, and a legalism that means that, where there is a doubt about the moral rightness of an action, the safe course of action is followed. It shows in the way in which some people looking at the morality of abortion, who are unable to decide when a foetus has moral worth, assume it is at the moment when the ovum is fertilised. That is safe.

It also shows in the way in which those who hold such a view of God sometimes behave towards others. The keeping of the moral law becomes all-important and they feel a responsibility to ensure that others keep it. It can lead to a hardness and coldness towards people who seem to be ignoring what they take to be the right moral standards and a concern for the observance of fixed forms of behaviour.

It is understandable that we might think of God as a hard, all-seeing taskmaster, for it is part of the traditional view of God that is passed from one generation to another as a way of motivating us to behave ourselves. It also has a measure of support from some Old Testament incidents. But it does not accurately reflect the God who calls us to live in right ways.

It is interesting that Christians sometimes reflect a view of God as judge in their law-driven behaviour, for God calls his people to show what he is like. God invites us to join him in the quest for a good society composed of good people. In taking up that invitation we will share something of his nature. This is the significance of the charge, 'Be holy because I, the Lord your God, am holy' (Leviticus 19:2). That is matched in the New Testament when Jesus gave his followers a way of *being* in his teaching and his life, and in passages like the Sermon on the Mount invited us to make this way of life our own. The apostle Paul took up the same theme. In writing to the Philippians, for example, having given them his moral exhortations he says that their attitude should be the same as that of Jesus Christ. He then goes on to describe Christ's servant nature (Philippians 2). In his letter to the Ephesians he repeats the charge, 'Be imitators of God, therefore, as dearly loved children and live a life of love' (Ephesians 5:1). The call to live a morally good life is a call to live lives that reflect the character of God and, in particular, to reflect it as we see him in Jesus Christ.

When the idea of a judging God becomes the main way in which he is seen, Christianity becomes a matter of law keeping and life is lived looking over one's shoulder at the great God who knows all we do, notes it down and will use it in evidence against us. Whatever the theological accuracy or inaccuracy of such an account, that is not the basis for the ethics that we find in the Bible.

But what is the key to the character of God? What is this essential feature of his being which he wishes men and women to reflect?

The God who Loves. **His character is fundamentally one of love**. That is what God *is*. It was John who, after spending so much time close to Jesus and listening to him, wrote in one of his letters, 'God is love. Whoever lives in love lives in God, and God in him' (1 John 4:16). Love is his very being. It was love that prompted his actions and it was his actions that expressed his love. 'When Israel was a child, I loved him, and out of Egypt I called my son' (Hosea 11:1). It was love that was behind him taking human form and being born as a child. 'For God so loved the world that he gave his one and only Son' (John 3:16). It is the love of God that calls us to respond in kind. 'We love because he first loved us. If anyone says, "I love God," yet hates his brother he is a liar' (1 John 4:19–20).

His love is depicted in biblical imagery. He is the good shepherd and the farmer who cares for his vineyard, the eagle that catches its young on its wings. Isaiah depicts him as a husband, 'The Lord will call you back as if you were a wife deserted and distressed in spirit – a wife who married young only to be rejected. For a brief moment I abandoned you but with deep compassion I will bring you back' (Isaiah 54:6–7).

In the same way that being a single male defines what a bachelor is, so God is defined as love. Just as a triangle has three angles and would not be a triangle without them, so God is love and the Christian God would not be God if he were not.

The basic characteristic of Christian ethics, then, is to be found in the nature of God which is love. Here is the basic principle from which all Christian ethics begins. It shapes the content of what is right and wrong, the intention of moral behaviour, and provides the motivation to live in accordance with the character of God.

The Ethics of a Relationship

The Old Testament. There is something strange about the moral codes in the Old Testament, particularly those described in the first five books. We have seen that they were not unique in what they have to say, but had their counterparts among other tribes in the area. Yet the Old Testament seems to give them a special place in the life of Israel that goes beyond a simple set of moral laws. This suggests that there is something significant about such laws, and indeed there is. The laws are the same but the significance is different. In the Old Testament they express a relationship between God and his people which theologians call the 'covenant'. The idea here is that God committed himself to Israel to be their God. That, in turn, invited a response that they acknowledge him as their God.

Although the form of words suggests that the moral codes are lists of rules and prohibitions, the relationship they express becomes clear when we look more closely at their context. When Moses received the Ten Commandments from God (Exodus 20) they were prefaced by the words, 'I am the Lord your God, who brought you out of Egypt, out of the land of slavery.' Then came the Commandments.

The preface sets the context for what God had to say to his people. The Commandments were not a set of rules laid down in a vacuum by an all-knowing and all-powerful God, with a demand that this particular group of people should obey him. Rather, he spoke of what he had done for them in bringing them out of slavery, and then he told them the appropriate response, which was to be his special people and to show this by keeping the moral codes.

In the previous chapter of Exodus we find the same idea: 'Then Moses went up to God, and the Lord called to him from the mountain and said, "This is what you are to say to the house of Jacob and what you are to tell the people of Israel: 'You yourselves have seen what I did to Egypt, and how I carried you on eagles' wings and brought you to myself. Now if you obey me fully and keep my covenant, then out of all the nations you will be my treasured possession . . .' These are the words you are to speak to the Israelites"' (Exodus 19:3–6).

Again, in Hosea 13, God's words are, 'But I am the Lord your God who brought you out of Egypt. You shall acknowledge no God but me, no Saviour except me.'

That act of deliverance was a sign of the love that God had for his people, and that invited them to be loyal and faithful to him and him alone, as their response. This idea of doing things as a loving response to what someone else has done is easy to understand. We feel a loyalty to our school or club as a response for what we have received there. Sportsmen are sometimes heard to say that they have got so much from their sport that they want to put something back into it. Many people feel a loyalty to their family. It may be hard to be precise about the reason, but part of it is that the love we receive from those close to us produces a response. People who do not experience much love in a family are often those who find it hardest to be loyal to it. So **one of the characteristics of Christian ethics is an invitation to respond to the love and goodness of God by being faithful to him**.

The role of the various moral codes, then, is to indicate what it means to respond in this relationship. We usually think of the moral code as being what we find in the Ten Commandments in Exodus 20, but that is only one formulation. There is another version in Deuteronomy 5:6–21 and similar, though not precisely the same, codes in Deuteronomy 27:15–26 and Leviticus 19:11–18. The thing they have in common is that they all show the appropriate way of life for those who are in the covenant.

It is like someone offering us a gift – a genuine gift, to which we wonder how we should respond. We could just say thank-you or perhaps better, we could support them in some way, not because we have been bribed, but because we appreciate the gift and want to respond to the kindness and generosity of the giver. We may wonder what an adequate appropriate response is. For Israel, the adequate response was to behave in the way described by the moral codes.

Some scholars believe that the commandments given after the Exodus had a special role to play in the history of Israel. We know that the people who left Egypt with Moses were not all descendants of Abraham. There were people from other tribes who were slaves in Egypt at the same time as the Israelites, and some of them took advantage of the situation to join the Exodus and escape. But they brought their own tribal gods and moral standards with them. The suggestion is that the Ten Commandments were a way of saying what it would mean if these people from other tribes seriously wanted to become part of God's community.

That makes a lot of sense because it explains why the Commandments contain both explicitly religious as well as moral requirements. It is as though they are saying to those who wish to join the covenant people, 'You have your own gods, but if you become part of God's community, "You shall have no other gods before me." You have worshipped idols, but now, "You shall not make for yourself an idol in the form of anything in heaven above or on the earth beneath or in the waters below. You shall not bow down to them or worship them; for I, the Lord your God, am a jealous God . . ." Your moral standards may have been marked by violence and self-interest, but they are not the way to respond to the love of God. Instead, "You shall not murder. You shall not steal."'

The moral requirements of the Old Testament, then, need to be seen as part of a relationship with God. At the heart of Old Testament ethics is a relationship within the Godhead. There is a relationship between God the Father, his Son and the Holy Spirit. He is a God who is relational in his very being, and this shows in his work of redemption through the Son and his comfort and teaching of men and women through the Holy Spirit. It is no wonder that the Ten Commandments and other moral requirements are relational, setting out the very basic minimum of an adequate response to God's love and goodness.

The consequence is that the moral codes are not a set of fundamental principles on which we can build a detailed moral code that will cover all eventualities, as has been suggested by some people, but rather, they are a broad guide to the kind of life expected of those who respond to the invitation of God to join his people in response to his love.

The New Testament. This Old Testament idea comes to its fulfilment in the New Testament where the message is the same. As John wrote in one of his letters, 'Since God so loved us, we also ought to love one another.' Again, 'We love because he first loved us' (1 John 4:11, 19). This identifies a basic motive for Christian moral behaviour, namely, that it is the proper response to the love and goodness of God shown in Jesus Christ. This is a far cry from the idea of the commandments being a series of impossible demands imposed by a distant and demanding God.

As an expression of a relationship with God ethics is not alone. It is a part of the wider response that God's love invites.

For purposes of separating things out, so that we can think more clearly about them, we identify ethics and worship, mission and spirituality. In practice they are all interrelated aspects of the way in which Christians follow Jesus.

At the heart of Christian ethics, then, is the relationship with God which we find in the Old Testament, and which is carried forward to a relationship with Jesus Christ.

Jesus at the Centre

Other moral codes may come with the teachings of great and wise men and women, and such people often have helpful things to say to us. Christian ethics does not come solely from the teaching of the lawgivers and prophets of the Old Testament and from Jesus Christ and his followers in the New, but from his life and death and resurrection. The reason is that his teaching is not to be separated from his person. **He is not just a teacher but the embodiment of all he said**, and that was confirmed in his resurrection from the dead. Without that it would all have been but words.

This is where people get it wrong when they claim that Jesus was simply a good moral teacher, or they equate the Christian faith with morality. There is a long tradition that links the Christian faith with morality, and rightly so. Some have gone so far as to claim that Christianity is fundamentally a moral position which is given authority by referring to an idea of God, and if that God is essentially seen as sitting in judgment on our behaviour, then there is a very strong motivational force for obedience to a moral code. That reduces Christianity to a moral stance and fails to do justice to the historical basis of the Christian faith and to the concept of responding in love to the love of God.

Nevertheless, the general direction of such a view is correct. Christianity has a strong moral element to it which is actually integral to its teaching and claims. Consider the claims that Christians make about God. He is seen to be the perfect one, and that applies to his moral nature as well as his person. If that is so then we would expect to find our moral standards in the words and actions of God. It is simply a matter of common sense, then, to look to the people who tell us about this perfect God, to find the moral standards for human beings.

In the case of the Christian religion there can be no doubt about the moral element in it. Indeed, for some people Christianity is synonymous with moral teaching such as the Ten Commandments and the Sermon on the Mount. It is noticeable that when there is national concern about the moral behaviour of young people, it is not unusual for there to be a demand for the teaching of the Ten Commandments. At various times in the past the teaching of Religious Education in schools has been defended on the grounds that it provides a good foundation for the teaching of morality.

This was expressed in a statement by the Earl of Selborne in a statement in the House of Lords in the debate on the 1944 Education Act which made Religious Education a compulsory subject in schools. He spoke of 'an England which avows as never before the principle of liberty, justice, toleration and discipline, on which this realm depends, and which themselves are founded on the teaching of the Church of Christ'.

The mistake in all this is to miss the significance of Jesus as the embodiment of God's way of life to which he calls people. It is a life that Jesus described as following him, not in the sense of accepting his teaching – other great leaders ask that – but of binding ourselves to him and finding in him – the person and work of Jesus of Nazareth – our way of life. That includes our attitudes to life, our lifestyle, our relationships with others and with the world in which we live. All this is personified in Jesus, rather than simply being found in a lot of teaching, or abstract principles which we have to apply, or in personal and social panaceas to be grasped at. **It is Jesus himself who is the unique standard of Christian ethics, not his ideas or even the principles he taught**.

In his book *Ethics and Christianity*, Keith Ward describes Jesus as the *exemplar* rather than an *example* of what it means to live this moral life. When we set good examples for our children we are illustrating something that can be known in other ways. There can be other examples. But when he speaks of Jesus as the exemplar, Keith Ward means that the moral way of life that is Christian can only be seen in Jesus. He embodies the right way of life and in him we are back to the source of what it is like to be a morally acceptable person.

The distinction between an example and an exemplar, as Ward uses the words, is that when we see Jesus as an example we imply there is some 'good' of which he is an example and of which there may be other examples. We may believe he is the best, even the perfect example, but he is still an example along with other good people.

Jesus as an Example

GOOD

Examples

Jesus
St A
Mr B
The Rev. C
Mrs D
Sister E

When Jesus is the exemplar, he himself is the 'good' and good people are examples of him:

Jesus as the Exemplar

JESUS

Examples

St A
Mr B
The Rev. C
Mrs D
Sister E

As an example he is one of many. He may be the best and the most consistent and authentic example, but he is still an example of goodness which is external to him. As an exemplar he is the embodiment of goodness of which others may be examples, for he is the embodiment of God.

There is a deceptive simplicity about Jesus which tempts us to look at the great moral statements he made and gladly nod our heads in approval. The Golden Rule, 'Do to others what you would have them do to you,' makes such sense. The Sermon on the Mount sets out what we may accept as a picture of an ideal world to which we ought to aspire. Loving our enemies, self-giving without seeking recompense or recognition, a willingness to forgive, are all very splendid, but we may think they are idealistic and other-worldly. We may well ask what they have to do with the realities of life in competitive business, or on the ward of a busy hospital, or coping with unruly children all day, or having to fight for recognition and promotion.

The answer is that their meaning is to be seen in Jesus, with all that happened to him. He has been there and done it. He has been through the mill and still, in what happened to him, lived the way of a life with God. His cause is the cause of God, and he is one with the Father. **It is in him that we find what is unique about Christian ethics**. This ethic is not just based on the requirement that we love one another, nor any other principle we can think of, nor any particular way of making our decisions, whether by rules or consequences or intentions. These things may be helpful and enhance the way in which people come to moral decisions, and pragmatically we may want to encourage what helps people to give shape to their lives. But they are not what makes an ethic Christian. That is Jesus. Jesus is obviously at the centre of ethics for the Christian – indeed, Christians can have no ethic save the Christian ethic.

That is the situation, then. We are invited to respond to the living God who loves us so much that he gave his Son. The response is not to a set of moral propositions, but to a person,

Jesus Christ, who embodied God's cause so that his way was God's way. This still begs the question of what our response should be to Jesus.

The Lordship of Christ

In his book *The Cost of Discipleship*, Dietrich Bonhoeffer, a German pastor who was killed for opposing Hitler, spoke of what following Jesus meant. He wrote, 'It is nothing else than bondage to Jesus Christ alone, completely breaking through every programme, every set of laws. No other significance is possible, since Jesus is the only significance. Beside Jesus nothing has any significance. He alone matters.' We are back to the idea of relationship, but for the Christian it is a living, dynamic relationship with God the Son, Jesus Christ.

Bonhoeffer's words point to our response in the relationship. It is one of accepting Christ's lordship and living our lives in that context. The mark of the Christian community is that it accepts the sovereignty of Jesus and tries to live under his rule. That the Christian community accepts his lordship is what makes it distinctive. To change the picture, we are members of the kingdom over which he rules, and so our lives are to portray our citizenship. This is why ethics takes its place with worship and mission and spirituality. They are all part of the response to him. This is what gives the ground on which Christians can judge their conduct. The questions to ask are, 'How consistent is the behaviour with the lordship of Jesus Christ?' or 'How appropriate is the response to his love that claims loyalty?'

Lordship is not always a very helpful image for Christian life. It can be taken to imply a mediaeval picture of an autocratic lord who has serfs and villains to do as he decrees. The picture of a slave was certainly used by the apostle Paul when he wrote to his friends. He described himself in that way in Romans 1:1 and Galatians 1:10, but it was a voluntary serfdom entered into out of love in response to the Lord. To speak of the lordship of Christ does not imply obeying commands to escape punishment, but to respond to his wishes.

In a television programme in 1997 it was claimed that some of the policies that developed in Nazi Germany were not formulated by Hitler, but by the people close to him. They made laws and authorised action on the basis of what they knew of his general views and attitudes. Whether this is true or not, it is close to the idea of being a slave of Christ's. Such slavery is a willing response to him, which seeks to express his will and share his attitudes.

How does this work out? One way is that we take Jesus as our moral model, but we need to be careful about what that means for us. Some people feel impelled to follow Jesus in his way of life, and so embrace poverty and give themselves to others in an obvious way. Mother Teresa was just one of thousands who seek to share the experiences of Christ. For most of us, though, we need to follow him in the chores of everyday life: looking after children, earning a living and trying to make a decent life for ourselves and the people for whom we have responsibility. That can be difficult, if only because there are so many things about which there is little or nothing specific about Jesus that we can use as a model.

Our imitation is not one that tries to match precisely what he did. It seems pointless even to try to do that because we live in a different environment from him and at a different time in history. We have problems that he did not have, simply because of the times in which we live. As far as we know he did not have to pronounce on birth control, yet in our time it is a matter of concern in some sections of the Church. He did not have to think about the rights and wrongs of test-tube babies. Nor did he have to decide where to invest his money.

Christian ethics is about responding in a relationship with the God who is love. Pre-eminently it is about responding to the person and work of Jesus and living in ways that reflect him as the one who embodies what human beings ought to be like.

The aspects of Christianity we have been thinking about are features of Christian theology, and illustrate the way in which theology and ethics are part of a whole in Christian thought.

Instead of talking of Christian ethics we could talk legitimately of moral theology, for the basis of this ethic is theological. So far we have thought about three aspects of theology:

- The fact that Christian ethical considerations start from a view of God as love.

- At the heart of Christian ethics is a relationship between God and human beings.

- For Christians Jesus is the very core of the Christian life as the exemplar of what is good. Christian ethics is about a relationship with him which results in a life that is faithful to him.

This is the starting point for an account of Christian ethics, and it is the crucially distinctive feature of living as a Christian.

10

Being Human

As we have seen, one starting point for Christian ethics is the nature of God as love. It is the response to this God, in particular as found in Jesus Christ, that marks Christian ethics as a distinctive way of shaping lives. There is another important starting point which is an integral part of our moral life, and this is the view we take of what it is to be human. The Christian sense of the importance of human beings is something that is shared with humanists, yet as we will see, the Christian viewpoint is justified and developed in a way that is distinctive.

We can see and evaluate what people do, so it is tempting to think that morality is about what people *do*. This was the assumption behind the discussion in Chapter 1 when we thought about Sophie's situation and discussed whether actions are intrinsically right or wrong. Yet this approach is only part of the concern of ethics.

Morality is also about people, as was suggested earlier in Chapter 5 when we thought about the community basis of ethics, an essential presupposition in ethics. The situations about which we make judgments in ethics are those in which people behave and think in certain ways: they involve attitudes that people have, and above all, the relationships they form with other people and with the world around them. We do not ascribe morality to animals. We do not say that it is immoral when a lion kills an antelope, or when a fox kills a chicken. Words like 'murder' that we would use of human behaviour just do not apply in such cases. Morality is about human beings and the way we relate to each other and to our world.

The role of human beings is of such importance that it has been suggested that the goal of life is to become the best that human beings can be. With this view, the job of ethics is to guide us to that goal. It is an attractive idea.

Theologically it has two sources. First, **the emphasis which is placed on the immediacy of Christian faith**. Far from seeing the kingdom of God as solely a future event, it recognises that the kingdom is here and now and that there is the possibility of a transformed life in the present with growth towards what we can become. Second, **the implication that we can identify what human beings are like at their best**, and here Christians claim we see that in Jesus Christ whom we have seen to be the exemplar of Christian life. This requires us to acknowledge his humanity fully, not just in relation to God, but to his fellow human beings. The role of ethics in this is that of a light to show us something of what this goal of full humanity looks like and the values and attitudes that are required to achieve it.

But in ethics there is more to the concept of humanity than offering an ideal to be achieved. Our humanity, as we experience it now, also has a part to play in the way in which we view moral life. The basic assumption that is shared by Christians and many non-Christians alike, is that human beings are of worth. It is the reasons for this worth and the implications for ethics that makes the Christian position distinctive.

Human Beings Are of Worth

The importance of human beings in the way we live together is recognised by both religious and non-religious bodies. The 1948 Universal Declaration on Human Rights asserts that 'these rights derive from the inherent dignity of the human person'. Article 1 asserts that human beings are 'born free and equal in dignity and rights'. What started as a concern for the dignity of persons, and the civil rights that followed from that, has been expanded into economic and social rights. The dignity of the person has been restated in documents in Africa, Asia and Latin America. In Europe it has found expression in the Council of Europe's Convention for Protection of Human Rights and Fundamental Freedoms (1950) and in the European Social Charter (1961). At a less formal level it is fundamental to the work of organisations such as Amnesty International as it seeks the release of political prisoners and the ending of cruelty and torture.

Christian bodies have made similar assertions about human worth. In their 1987 study, *Changing Britain: Social Diversity and Moral Unity*, the Church of England Board for Social Responsibility came to the conclusion that 'Morality . . . is essentially a matter of respect for persons and the necessary conditions for their flourishing.' In the same vein the Roman Catholic document, *Acta Synodalia Concilii Vaticani II*, states that 'Human activity must be judged insofar as it refers to the human person integrally and adequately considered.'

The respect for persons and for human dignity that we find in numerous official documents depends on an underlying belief that human beings are of great value. We are worth relating to and it is worth considering how best we should relate with one another.

Try to imagine what it would be like to live in a land where distinctions between right and wrong are unknown and there is simply no reflection on human behaviour at all. Such a place would probably be just a collection of individuals from whom possessions could be taken at will, where the weak could be exploited and bullied, where there would be no restraint on sexual appetites, where children could be abused, and where the strong could have their own way at the expense of the weak. It would be a thoroughly nasty place simply because there would be no felt need for restraint, other than that which would enable people to survive.

Fortunately, even though there are instances when people do behave like this, our world does have restraints. As a general rule we accept that human beings are of some worth and that means they are to be protected. At the very least most of us believe we ourselves are of worth. In practice we learn that others too are of worth. From the time that we are small children we discover that if we do not treat others in generally acceptable ways, we suffer. Other people tend to react to what we do to them. If we treat them badly, then, in return, they may treat us badly, and we do not like that. Sometimes we reflect on our experiences and see that there is a certain logic in thinking that if I am of worth, then there is no obvious reason why others are not of similar worth.

The good news the Church has to offer presents a distinctive view of this worth. Such a sense of worth is not merely dependent on the practical realities of living a trouble-free life together. The Christian claim is that we are of great worth because in God's eyes we are lovable without limits. In his Gospel John wrote that God loved the world so much that he gave his one and only Son in order that, in some way, we might have a full life. The good news is that this is true no matter how bad we are or how deep-rooted is the evil we might perpetrate. The cost of giving his innocent Son to the ignominy of a cross for us is beyond imagination, but this is the worth of human beings to God, and the cross is evidence of that worth. It is good news that God's love recognises the depths to which we can sink, yet, even so, he still loves us: the unlovely who would reject his love. God, then, must have a very high view of our worth.

There is a mistaken idea among some Christians that this worth only extends to the soul and that the body is of less worth. It stems from a belief that we are made up of two parts, body and soul, the most important of which is the soul. It sometimes results in some Christians believing that we ought to rise above our physical pleasures and senses and to dominate our physical desires. It is true that these desires need keeping under control so that we do not live solely for their gratification, but this is not to deny their worth as some would have us do. Our physical appetites are part of who we are as men and women who matter to God, and if we are to respect ourselves then we are to respect our bodies and the sensual side of our nature. Jesus had a body. He was God made flesh and we have no reason to doubt that he enjoyed his physical body. Life can be physically good, whether it is the pleasure of a little girl skipping down the path, or the trial of strength in a rugby scrum, or the pleasure of the wind on the face on a walk in the mountains. Life can be enhanced by our bodies and their pleasures are part of enjoying being a person created by God.

Similarly, we have minds to stretch and imaginations with which to envisage fresh possibilities and dream dreams. We have the ability to be creative with our hands and minds, to produce beautiful objects and to startle and stimulate each other with new ideas. We have the capacity to relate to each other and enjoy the company of those around us as we express our nature as social beings. It is all part of being human as Jesus was human, and part of the worth of being human.

Made in God's Image. Some Christians want to restrict most of their sense of worth to the way in which God works out human salvation: he loves us so much that he saves us. But the same worth is also to be found in the biblical view of creation. The creation stories are not there to provide a scientific account of how things began. They tell us that right from the beginning human beings were made in God's own image. To bear that image gives us great worth. To be made in his image means that we were made to be like God in some way, and we must be special for that to be so. It means that God loves not just those who want to please him, but the whole of created humanity – warts and all! We must be of worth if he does that.

We have already noticed one of the notable biblical examples of this sense of worth in action when we thought of Amos' plea for justice for the poor. Behind the demands of the Old Testament for justice is a concern that the worth of every person is recognised and respected. They tell of God's concern that the poor be treated fairly, and the implication is that they matter too much to be the victims of a corrupt legal system. Perhaps it is the sense of worth that makes people who are denied justice sometimes feel they do not have a place in society. They feel demeaned as persons. Yet as part of God's creation, made in his image, they are of such worth that their well-being and their dignity ought to be respected. It means that there is something about us, in our very humanity, that imposes on each of us an obligation to treat others fairly and with dignity.

So a fundamental assumption of ethics, as Christians understand the enterprise, is that human beings are of worth. How we treat each other matters, then, whether we do it within a framework of what we call Christian ethics or in secular ethics.

An example of the way in which a failure to keep this sense of human worth to the fore can affect our thinking is to be found in the view that in some extreme cases, there are people who act in such a totally immoral and unacceptable way that they distance themselves from the rest of us, and we no longer have any obligation to behave in morally right ways towards them. This is an argument that is sometimes used to justify the way in which the Hebrew midwives lied to Pharaoh (Exodus 1:15–22). Pharaoh ordered them to kill the male babies of the Hebrews, but the women disobeyed. When he wanted to know why they were not doing as he said, they lied to him and said that the births took place before they got to the mothers. The claim is that Pharaoh was such an evil man that he was beyond the women's moral obligation to tell the truth.

At times we may certainly feel that way about people. Did some of the tyrants of this century such as Hitler or Stalin deserve to be treated in a morally acceptable way? Did the Nazis deserve any mercy after their treatment of the Jews? When, fifty years after the event, we find war criminals who directly caused the deaths of innocent people, ought we to show mercy after such a length of time, or ought we to insist on justice being done? Or when it becomes possible to apply for the extradition of an elderly, sick train-robber, ought it to be sought for the sake of justice, or should we show mercy after such a length of time? Our emotions may say there should be no mercy when the crimes have caused the death of others, but our emotions are notoriously unreliable guides to what is right and wrong and can certainly get in the way of what is just. Such cases can be a problem.

In the case of Pharaoh, perhaps we need to reflect further on the nature of our God before we say he was beyond our moral obligation. God recognises the worth and dignity of all human beings and it is difficult to accept that any of us can reach the point when we do not deserve respect. This is not to say that justice ought not to be done, but to say that to put someone beyond a moral obligation on our part is hard to square with belief in the Christian God. Indeed, it is the basis of the Christian doctrine of grace that God acts in love in spite of what we do. God's people have a moral obligation to follow their God in their love, and traditionally Christians have accepted that there are no reservations about it.

Human Beings Are Not Perfect

Another reason why Christian ethics is bound up with humanity and what it is to be human is that Christians believe there are various human factors that prevent us attributing worth to each other. Christians often put those factors together when they describe all human beings as sinners. If our human worth is to be acknowledged there needs to be some way of minimising the effects of sin, with all the resulting hurt and damage that we cause ourselves and others. It is for this reason that we need an ethical system to guide us in how to act towards each other. We need some way of establishing right from wrong.

The human condition that we call sin, and which Christians see as originating in Adam's act of rebellion against God, finds expression in at least three ways among Christians and non-Christians alike:

- We all have a distorted view of God.

- We are all victims of sin.

- We are all damaged people.

We All have a Distorted View of God. One of the leaders of the early Church, called Athanasius, realised that one of the major effects of sin is that we are unable to see things in the right perspective because we do not see God properly. We have distorted ideas of him and because of that we do not recognise what he has to say about the kind of people he would like us to be. When Jesus was walking this earth he found this distortion very evident in the Pharisees who laid down in great detail what the Law of Moses meant and what should be done to keep it. For example, they taught what they believed the Law implied about what could and could not be done on the Sabbath, even to the point of saying how far people could walk. The minutiae made God's way of living into a great burden which they believed God demanded of them. Yet it was a distortion.

The writer to the Hebrews realised what was happening, not just with the Pharisees but with us all as we make God in our own image. He started his letter by writing, 'In the past God spoke to our forefathers through the prophets at many times and in various ways, but in these last days he has spoken to us by his Son.' People had not got the message. They had failed to understand what God was saying, so he became man. God is like Jesus, and now that we have seen Jesus we have seen the Father.

But still those whose ethical system is Christian do not grasp what our heavenly Father is like. We want him to act and react as we would. We want him to condemn what we would condemn and approve of what we would approve. The problem with this – let us call it 'sin' – is that we pass it on to others and impose our burdens and warped ideas about God on to them. Sometimes we give this a religious slant and say we want to do what our religion tells us to; at other times we do it because we want life to be to our advantage. Either way it results in a failure to give others the worth that is their due.

We Are All Victims of Sin. One of the reasons we behave in ways that are hurtful is that we learn our behaviour from those around us, and we do what we think other people want us to do. There are pressures upon us to do so. We learn values from our parents and those we admire, and then our children learn their values from us – even those values that are not made explicit. A ten-year-old boy is quite likely to share his parents' views about those of other races, and then in turn pass them on to others.

But the problem is more than just being the victim of others' values. We are also victims of each others' anger and pride. Children soon learn when it is going to be acceptable to be truthful, but they also learn that admitting they were not where their parents thought they were will get them into trouble, and that is something to be avoided. So the lie is told – not necessarily because they want to tell it, but because they are the victim of a parent's anger. We are the victims of the sins of others, and sometimes that influences the way we behave.

We Are All Damaged People. Another way of describing this is to say that we are damaged. In various ways and for various reasons we carry the marks of the past. As we understand more of the effects of our upbringing and experiences, so we recognise more of the fears and defence mechanisms, hang-ups and false faces we have developed to help us cope with life. It is because we are 'damaged goods' that some of us behave the way we do. For example, because of parental drive and expectations in our youth, we may not be able to handle failure in our lives. To that extent our past affects who we are today and contributes to the way we behave in order to avoid failure.

This element of damage to our humanity can affect us in a variety of ways. Some people become outrageously irrational. Some become defensive, while others see the world as a place marked by changes, each of which is a threat to the status quo with which they feel comfortable. Some commit acts that to the rest of us may appear to be morally wrong, while others are victims of a lack of love and find it hard to find an identity.

Our damaged humanity means that as we look at what others do in their lives we perceive with a flawed judgment. Some of us love to criticise people, even when we do not know what makes them behave as they do. We see the external outcomes of a damaging past and a flawed, pressured present. We just do not know what makes others behave as they do, even as they do not know what causes us to do what we do, yet we feel able to judge one another.

We are in a chain that affects the way we behave, whether we like it or not. Yet at the same time it is within this chain that we learn what is right and wrong. We learn from people and respond to our environment in ways that will protect our sense of well-being. The result is that those who follow Jesus Christ in wanting to give due worth to others, need the guidance and direction that an ethical stance can give. Jesus broke that chain in that, not having a distorted view of God, he neither passed on a distorted view of God, nor the distorted values and responses of a damaged victim of sin. But we are not Jesus, and it is one of the assumptions of ethics that we need help in handling the problems of a life where we are victims.

Human Beings Live in Communities

Human beings live in communities. They may be huge conurbations or small hamlets, but normally we live alongside others. One of the results of this is that we become interdependent and look to each other for support and help. We become increasingly aware of our interdependence. Whether it is the need for information that others have, or for the delivery of the groceries from the depot to the supermarket, or the skills of doctors and paramedics, teachers, vets or the golf pro, we look to each other to make life at least tolerable. In the familiar words of John Donne: 'No man is an island, entire of itself; every man is a piece of the continent, a part of the main; if a clod be washed away by the sea, Europe is the less, as well as if a manor of thy friends or thine own were; any man's death diminishes me, because I am involved in mankind; and therefore never send to know for whom the bell tolls; it tolls for thee' (*Devotions upon Emergent Occasions* (1624), Meditation XVII). Or, as Martyn Harris wrote more recently:

> And beneath that again, and deeper still, there seems to lie a recognition of connectedness and mutuality. I cannot function properly in society as an atom of pride and self-interest. I cannot survive in the universe as a chunk of matter randomly generated by impersonal physical laws. I have to hand myself over to the idea that I am reciprocally connected to other people and to the universe in ways I cannot understand and have humbly to accept. And that, in far too many words, is what I think I mean by love.
> ('Something Understood', *Daily Telegraph*, 25 May 1996)

It is not just that we need each other as individuals. Nations need each other. Some have grain and others oil. Some have financial and business expertise and others have developed technical skills. The people of some countries go hungry and need those nations which have food in abundance. At another level too we need each other. A political system which has no effective opposition is dangerous because it is open to abuse and corruption. The State in the form of a ruling power needs individuals and interest groups to challenge and voice their dissent, if it is to be a State in which truth is respected and sought.

The importance of these interdependent needs lies in the fact that life is complex and if we are to have a moral life, whether in community or as individuals, we need other people from whom we can learn and with whom we can explore ideas about the kind of world we want and the kind of people we want to be. It is when we stop listening to others that we become prejudiced, selfish and arrogant and our moral life is diminished.

This interdependence is not a social convenience. It is part of being human that we are social beings. We need each other if we are to grow and reflect more of our true humanity, and for this reason we have a responsibility to work against those things that will divide and prevent us from recognising each other's worth and acting interdependently.

This is another reason why we need an ethical system that will enable us to live in such a way. Because we live in community we need to recognise what is right and wrong and so acknowledge that people matter.

Human Beings Are to Love Themselves

Loving ourselves is something that secular ethics recognises, as should those who start from a Christian point of view. In Christian ethics, however, respecting the humanity in others is one thing, Christians respecting their own humanity is often another, particularly for busy people who have a strong desire to serve others, or to get to the top of their profession.

Jesus's response to the question of what is the greatest commandment, was love for God and 'love your neighbour as yourself'. Over the years there have been different suggestions as to what he meant by this. For example, did he mean we are to love others to the same extent that we love ourselves? Or perhaps he meant 'love your neighbour in addition to loving yourself'. In both of these explanations there is an acceptance that Jesus is advocating self-love.

For some Christians, this is a major problem because they believe that the idea of loving ourselves is contrary to the teaching of the New Testament. Jesus spoke of a need to take up our cross and follow him, and of losing our life for him in order to save it (Mark 8:34–5). He also spoke of laying down his life for his friends (John 15:13). When the apostle Paul wrote of love in his letter to the Corinthians he said it was not self-seeking (1 Corinthians 13:5). Again, when he wrote to the Philippians he said that Jesus 'humbled himself and became obedient to death – even death on a cross' (Philippians 2:8). In the light of such statements it is reasonable to be suspicious of self-love.

Some Christians have a much stronger view of self-love. They believe that it is a natural trait of men and women to love themselves and this is the core of sin. It is self-love that prevents us loving God, and self and God are seen as two opponents in the fight for the allegiance of human beings. On this basis self-love is seen as evil.

Christians do not have to be so negative about self-love. As we have seen, human beings are made in the image of God and still carry that image however spoilt and blurred it might be. Thus each individual is of worth, and hence worth loving, not just by God and other people but by themselves.

We do not have to see self-love in a totally negative way, nor indulge it. There is a right and wrong way of loving ourselves. If self-love means being self-centred at the expense of loving God and the people around us, then it is certainly not a positive part of Christian ethics. If, however, it means a healthy regard for self that recognises the good things about being human, then it is something to be celebrated and enjoyed.

This need for a healthy self-regard certainly matches our experiences. If we did not love ourselves we would not care about our appearance or our health. If we have low self-esteem, why bother? There is a further practical consideration. Unless we learn to love ourselves we are unable to love others. A healthy self-love means that we have the confidence to look outside ourselves to the benefit of others.

Recognising our human worth, then, leads to a self-love that is realistic about the kind of people we are. That, in turn, leads to an ability to love others, which is morally good. If self-love becomes selfish then it is not of moral worth.

Healthy self-love has three obvious implications. First, self-love is a common need and **part of our responsibility to others is to help them grow in self-esteem**. At times we all, irrespective of our beliefs about God, need encouragement and someone to tell us that we are worth loving. All too often we give each other negative signals and emphasise what we are not, and while we need to be realistic we also need these tokens of acceptance and worth that tell us that we can love ourselves because we are lovable.

Second, **we need to give ourselves space**. Self-love can mean legitimately saying 'no' to some of the demands people make on us, at times even the demands of our immediate family. It is about claiming who we are in the eyes of God, made in his image to enjoy him and our fellow human beings. In a world where so many measure themselves in terms of the work they can do or the position they can attain, our humanity can become diminished and we need to reclaim it.

Third, **loving ourselves may also mean protecting ourselves from experiences that may cause us harm**. For example, an increasing number of people seem to allow themselves to live under stress, with the possible result of impaired health. That, in turn, results in an inability to function as they would wish. Christians, too, put themselves under pressure, and when it happens in the interests of the Church they sometimes see it as a mark of the extent of their dedication to their faith. They justify it with statements like, 'I would rather burn out than rust out' – as though God really wants a 'burnt out' people!

This is not to say that in protecting ourselves from harm we can opt out of difficult situations, but is simply to point out something of the implication of being lovable. We need to take care of ourselves if we are to be the people we might be.

Human beings are special people, then. And they are special not just because they are human and have certain anatomical characteristics that other animals lack. The Christian claim is that being human is to be made in the image of God and, as such, human beings are of worth. In this chapter, however, we have seen three things associated with human worth that affect ethics:

- A number of factors that prevent us from attributing worth to others as we should, are sin, a distorted view of God and being victims of sin (the fact that we are damaged people).

- Because we live in communities we need an ethical system to enable us to recognise the worth of others.

- We also have a responsibility to express our own self-worth.

11

Who Do I Want to Be?

In the story of Sophie's adultery we looked at the dilemmas a number of people had in deciding how to react to her behaviour. They were looking at two moral problems: how they ought to view Sophie's behaviour and how they ought to respond. They were asking **what was the right thing to do**, both for Sophie and for themselves, and that is the question we usually ask about human behaviour.

Christian ethics, however, goes deeper than merely responding to a given situation and deciding what to do about it: it asks questions about **what kind of person we want to be, or to become,** and **what attitudes we ought to have to life**. These are equally part of our moral decision making and as we will see, they are more basic to a Christian view of moral life.

This distinction, between what ought to be done and the kind of person we want to be, has long been recognised in Christian ethics. Just as there is a long tradition of dealing with principles and rules which are then applied to specific situations, there is an equally long tradition that ethics is about the kind of people Christians are. It is about character: what we should *be* rather than what we should *do*.

Over the years, Roman Catholic moral thinking has been more concerned with character and virtue than Protestant thinking has. But in recent years there has been a recognition among Protestants too that being is at least as important as doing.

In this chapter we are going to think about the decision-making process involved in being the kind of person we want to be and become.

God's Kind of Person

Sometimes we recognise how our character shows itself in what we do. Think about Helen. She is in a difficult marriage where her relationship with her husband is bearable, but very strained. They have simply drifted apart and her husband has made it clear that he does not want to improve the situation. The marriage is empty of affection and they no longer communicate with one another any more than they have to. Even though they go through the motions of behaving like a married couple in public, and though they get along without any more disagreements than other couples seem to have, Helen feels that the marriage has died. She has talked things over with a friend, who suggested that they should both be realistic and go their separate ways. However, they have two small children who think the world of their father, and Helen is conscious that they will be very hurt if she and her husband part. When she talked the matter over with another friend Helen asked her what she thought of the possibility of a separation. Her friend's answer was, 'But that is not the kind of thing you would do.' Helen realised it would be out of character for her to disrupt her family in that particular situation, even though her marriage was difficult.

Harry worked in a large organisation. At a departmental meeting his immediate boss announced a reorganisation of the department, and was insistent that the new scheme be put into place immediately. Like many others, Harry realised that it was an ill-considered proposal that would cause a lot of unrest and hurt unless there was a great deal of preparatory work done. Harry was the one who argued against the changes in that form. The scheme was delayed, but the result was that his boss took some of Harry's most rewarding work from him.

Two of Harry's colleagues were talking about it and agreed that he was being victimised and should complain to one of the assistant managers. But as one of them remarked about Harry, 'He will not do anything because he is not like that.' He was right. Harry was not like that.

We sometimes talk about a person showing character when we mean that they show some quality which is a strength in their lives. It may be something like integrity or consistency which they show in the way they deal with life, and in particular when they face difficulties.

At some time we may be asked for a character reference for someone. They want to know what the person is like. They are not talking about one-off reactions to life, but the kind of consistent responses that show the underlying values and moral qualities that the person has. The request is for information about the person's dispositions to act in certain ways. In our examples Helen could well have threatened to leave her husband. That would have been a one-off reaction. But she has a disposition not to harm people, and particularly her children and husband, and that affects what she does and does not do. Harry has a disposition not to complain and make a fuss, but to accept what happens to him. That reflects his character, though at some time he may well act out of character and storm in to have a row with his boss. That would be quite untypical of him and we would say it is out of character.

Our character is important when we are considering Christian ethics. What Jesus said in the Sermon on the Mount is, in part, a statement of the kind of dispositions that are appropriate for those who want to follow him. It is a statement about the kind of people we are if we genuinely accept Jesus's view of life and his set of priorities: 'Blessed are the poor in spirit . . . the meek . . . those who hunger and thirst for righteousness . . . the merciful . . . the pure in heart . . . the peacemakers' (Matthew 5:3–10).

The Christian way of life is one of reconciliation and forgiveness, a way in which enemies are to be loved. It is a life in which our acts of kindness are not proclaimed from the rooftop, a way that is not judgmental (Matthew 7:1–5). People who follow such a way illustrate what Jesus talked about when he said that the heart is the place from which come immoral actions (Matthew 15:17–20). We can sum up this way of life by saying that the Christian life is not simply about external behaviour but about the person we are.

The apostle Paul gave his friends in Galatia a picture of the kind of person Christians ought to be, when he wrote about the fruit to be expected of those who live by the Spirit of God. He gave an idea of conduct that is inappropriate, such as idolatry, drunkenness, orgies, fits of rage. He also gave an indication of the kind of people he wanted to contrast the Christian character with. They are those who are marked by hatred, selfish ambition, jealousy, dissensions, envy. It is against that background that he said, 'But the fruit of the Spirit is love, joy, peace, patience, kindness, goodness, faithfulness, gentleness and self-control. Against such things there is no law' (Galatians 5:22–3).

That is the kind of person who lives with the Spirit. Such qualities are the dispositions – the habitual characteristics – of the person who wants to live in the ways of God.

They do not tell us much about the way we ought to work out what love means in the situation we will face tomorrow, nor what goodness and kindness will entail. But then Paul is not setting out particular actions for us, nor is he laying down principles. He was writing about the kind of people his friends would be when their characters were formed by the Holy Spirit.

Character, then, is an integral part of what it means to live by a Christian ethic. Indeed, Christian ethics is not a matter of having a list of things to be done and things that are prohibited. The requirement of Christian ethics is to be a particular sort of person in our relationships and our view of the world. It is about our beliefs, values and attitudes, rather than rules and regulations, and in so far as it affects feelings and understanding, it affects the whole person.

Being and Doing

Although we have said that Christian ethics is about character, we cannot separate that from the way in which we behave. We do not know what a person's character is unless there is evidence of it, and that has to be evidence of repeated behaviour. Jesus once said, 'By their fruit you will recognise them' (Matthew 7:16). Actions are the way in which our character shows, though character is more than actions. It is also about those habits of thought, attitude and resolve which make up our disposition so that we behave in certain ways.

The moral choices we make come, not from sets of rules or principles, but from what we are as people. It is our character that gives the general direction to the things we do. We often say things like, 'I could never do that,' meaning that we could never act in certain ways. Some ways of behaving are foreign to us as persons. We do not try to apply principles, or analyse why. We simply know that it is not 'us'.

This means that our lives are largely directed by the kind of people we are, and that can lead to both good and bad results. Often the outcome is good, as in the case of Helen. Sometimes it is destructive, as, for example, where we have such a strong disposition to see that moral standards are observed that we become scrupulous. We become overanxious to see that everything is exactly right. It is not unusual for Christians to become like this. The result may be that they lose their inner freedom and become legalistic.

The value we place on our own character and the kind of character we have depends upon the kind of beliefs we hold. As we have seen, Christians hold to the beliefs of the Christian community and who they become ought, if they are consistent, to reflect the values and the attitudes which that community provokes. Who they become will in turn be reflected in their behaviour. Behind it all ought to

be a loyalty to Jesus Christ, whether the outcome is con-
genial or not.

Intentions as Guides

As we read earlier in Chapter 2, our intentions may play a part
in our decision making and in taking certain actions. So they
also play a role in being a Christian. Intentions are like the
flashlights that guide us into a dark building. They help us see
the way forward from where we are now. Logically they come
from the goals we have, the general perspective we have of life,
and, in turn, point us back towards them. That is certainly true
of moral life.

When we look at Christian ethics, and being 'a Christian',
there have been a number of ways these goals and intentions
have been expressed. One way is to speak of a desire to advance
the kingdom of God, which means living under the rule of
Christ and seeking his rule in all things. Sometimes people
express their intentions as being faithful to Jesus. Another way
of expressing it is to talk about seeking the glory of God in all
we do, or about fulfilling the will of God, or 'having the mind
of Christ' is yet another way of expressing it.

However we express our goals and intentions, from the point
of view of Christian ethics two things need emphasising. First,
it is about seeing the world through God's eyes. Second,
**Christians ought to be committed to Jesus Christ as the
Lord and exemplar of their moral life**. That is the framework
for Christian morality.

Developing Character

So, as a Christian wanting to live by a Christian ethical system,
you may be asking a question that non-Christians might also
ask, 'How do we become the people we want to be or become,
as Christians?' It is impossible to be specific because there
is no formula that we can lay down which simply needs
applying.

It would be foolish to try to compile a 'programme for character development'. To attempt such a thing would be a failure to recognise that the ways in which we grow as people are often unstructured. It is often the unexpected contacts with individuals or groups, or unforeseen experiences, that prove to be transforming. They cannot be programmed into our lives. As Christians, however, we can recognise some of the factors that may be at work.

First, **there may be specific experiences which form certain attitudes and qualities in us**. A good example is disappointment, and even pain. One of the ways we may try to comfort someone who has just failed an important examination is by telling them that failure is good for the character. Paul spoke of this when he wrote to the Romans, 'We also rejoice in our sufferings, because we know that suffering produces perseverance; perseverance, character; and character, hope' (Romans 5:3–4). Certainly, experiences of bereavement or near death can have a profound effect on us, sharpening our perception of the world and changing our values.

Second, **we may come into contact with other people who exemplify the qualities we want and admire**. Sometimes we know in principle what we want to be like, but it is through contact with a person who exemplifies it that the whole idea is given direction. At other times we have no previous desire to be anything in particular, but then we meet someone who has certain qualities we find attractive and we want to be like them. In a Christian context the example will be someone who exemplifies Christ.

Third, **we may find that our theology or other belief system points us in the direction of becoming a particular sort of person**. In other words, what we mentally come to believe helps to make us what we are. It could be a realisation that until that time we have seen Christianity more in terms of doing and now recognise that it is also about being. It is not unusual for Christians to be unclear about the detail of what they believe, but there are times when they have a flash of understanding that may lead them to pay attention to the person they are.

Fourth, **devotion to Jesus may lead people to want to be like him**. It is a matter of imitating him, not in what they do, but in the way they approach life. It is the willingness to accept rejection and misunderstanding, to be meek and lowly, to love to the limit.

It is here that the Bible is important as the record of God revealed pre-eminently in Christ. It is in those pages that we find Jesus as a model of humanity, and see his compassion and acceptance of those whom others rejected. We discover how he handled the prospect of power and fame. We also find him facing suffering and see his response to the damaging arrogance of the religious leaders of the time.

Yet discovering the man Jesus in the New Testament is not a process we can describe in detail. Knowledge of Jesus is likely to be gained through the different aspects of the Gospel accounts: the stories he told, his dealing with people such as the woman at the well at Sychar, his reception of the adulteress, what he said on the hillside, the temptations he faced, the events of that last week of his life, his time with his disciples. Whatever the specific content, it is likely to be an accumulation of images and teachings and impressions of Jesus that begins to form priorities for life and influences the directions we take.

Other biblical incidents or personalities may also affect what we are. It could be the devotion of the Psalms or the vision of the Church that is offered by the writers of the Epistles, but whatever and whoever it is, the Bible is full of events and people who may help to form who and what we are.

Experience of the Bible may affect people in changing theological perceptions and that, in turn, changes what they become. For example there may be a change in the way God is seen. That can make an enormous impact. There may be a realisation that the way humanity was previously perceived has been misguided and does not match the way men and women really are. That too can be of profound influence. It may be a simple overall unspecified impression that present experience is not what life should be like. Often the impact is indirect. We cannot say what the influence will be, but a change in perception happens and people are changed with it. It may be a soaking up of these transforming values and dispositions, rather as a sponge placed in a bowl of water soaks it up.

There is no single aspect of the Bible that can be programmed to transform us. Given that the exemplar of what it is to be God's kind of person is Jesus, it follows that time spent with his story is likely to be the sharpest influence, but that is not to say that it is the only influence, nor that it will be any particular aspect of what is known about him that will have the greatest influence.

The point is that whatever biblical material has an impact on us, the Bible can shape beliefs and attitudes and help to form dispositions. The prerequisite is that there is a willingness to be open to Scripture, and particularly to the story of Jesus.

Changing the Approach

There is a very important implication of seeing Christian ethics in terms of character. As we saw at the start of this chapter the recognition that ethics is about the persons we are changes the basic moral question. Thus far we have thought about some ways in which we might answer the question, '**What ought I to do?**' That leads us to a concern to find answers to the question, '**Is this action morally right?**' In this chapter we have asked, '**What kind of person ought I to be?**' The basic question now becomes, '**Is this action consistent with who I am and who I want to become?**'

This is a question far more in keeping with the New Testament idea of morality than asking what acts are wrong or right. 'Is this action morally right?' is the question we usually ask each other. The New Testament writers were more interested in Christians becoming a particular sort of person. Examples abound: 'As a prisoner of the Lord, then, I urge you to live a life worthy of the calling you have received' (Ephesians 4:1). 'Since, then, you have been raised with Christ, set your hearts on things above, where Christ is seated at the right hand of God. Set your minds on things above, not on earthly things. For you died, and your life is now hidden with Christ in God. When Christ, who is your life, appears, then you will also appear with him in glory. Put to death, therefore, whatever belongs to your earthly nature . . .' (Colossians 3:1). In Romans 6, after speaking of the believer being united with Christ in his death and resurrection, Paul writes, 'In the same way, count yourselves dead to sin but alive to God in Christ Jesus. Therefore do not let sin reign in your mortal body so that you obey its evil desires.' In other words, be what you are!

The apostle Peter is another writer who links what Christians are with the way they ought to behave. He writes, 'For you have been born again, not of perishable seed, but of imperishable, through the living and enduring word of God . . . Therefore, rid yourselves of all malice and all deceit, hypocrisy, envy, and slander of every kind' (1 Peter 1:23; 2:1).

There is, then, a repeated theme that Christians ought to behave morally, in ways that are consistent with what they are theologically.

So the basic question changes. **'Is this action morally right?'** enables us to stand away from situations. We are spectators who pass judgment on the way the game is being played. **'Is this act consistent with who I am and who I want to become?'** makes us players. It has what some see as the drawback of lacking the objectivity of what is deemed morally right. A successful search for actions that are right implies a certainty that is not present when a person is looking inwards at themselves. Yet it does not have to be like that at all. It would be mistaken to assume that **'who I am and who I want to become'** is simply a matter of personal choice. To ask the question in a moral context is to imply that there are criteria as to what a good person is like. In the case of Christian ethics those criteria revolve around the person of Jesus Christ and he is the measure of what Christian ethics requires we become.

We have seen how vital a role character can have in Christian ethics. As we discovered in Chapter 4, Christians can be very much like many other people in society when it comes to the things they do. The most obvious difference is likely to be in their character. In the character of Jesus there is something that goes against the normal way of behaving and reacting. In him what counted as important in the way he reacted to people and situations was quite different from our normal responses to life.

Because it is so fundamental to other moral questions and reflects the New Testament concept so much better than a search for right acts, the changed question we need to ask, which is basic to Christian ethics, is, **'Who am I and who do I want to become?'**

12

Decision Making

Whatever we might think is the correct ethical theory to hold, whether we believe that morality is basically decided by rules, or by the consequences of our actions, or by an allegiance to an ideology of God, there comes a time when we have to take some decisions. What ought we to do in practice? Life is full of situations that leave us uncertain about what to do.

Just before the fall of the Communist regimes in Eastern Europe, it became possible to cross the border into Hungary and from there move into the West. It was a wonderful way of escape for those who had longed for such a thing, and many took advantage of it. For others it presented a dilemma. They were among those able to make the journey and, having skills in professions such as medicine, were likely to find work in the West. But they feared what would happen in their home countries if such professional people left. It was a new situation and there was no knowing what the future held for them, but whatever the difficulties and tensions decisions had to be made and those concerned had to accept responsibility for what they did.

Ethics and Accountability

This idea of being responsible is important in ethics, for unless we are accountable for what we do, at least in some measure, it is difficult to see how we can attach moral praise or blame. We would be like animals or robots of which there are no moral expectations at all. The way we understand what morality means entails that we must assume that we are accountable for our actions. It is an important assumption in ethical thought, for without it there would be no moral enquiry at all.

This is not to say that it is an easy concept to understand, or that everyone agrees that we are accountable. It has become an unfortunate joke that social workers protect us from the consequences of our actions by blaming the environment or our upbringing. It is a sad joke because it tends to detract from all the good work these professionals do, but there is a strong element of truth in what is said. We are to a large extent the product of our past and circumstances. For example, the range of opportunities in life are in some measure determined by where we lived in our early years and the education that was available in that area. Our lack of success at an early stage can affect our motivation to achieve in later life. We can do much to overcome such difficulties and many do, but that does not alter the fact that our background and circumstances tend to limit what we can do. It is also true that our job opportunities are in part determined by our education, temperament, looks and even by our size if we want jobs as ballet dancers or guardsmen. In America it is said that anyone is free to become president, but that is a formal freedom. In practice it is limited to those with the necessary skills and financial backing. The truth is that there are some choices in life that are beyond our reach and we are not free to take them. Regrettably in some cases such limitations are taken as reasons for denying a person's worth, an idea which, as we saw earlier, is rejected in Christian ethics.

The debate this has caused over the years is enormous. Do we have free will, or are we determined? Are we conditioned in the way that animals can be conditioned to behave in certain ways, or are we capable of making genuine free decisions about the kind of life we lead? It is only in so far as we are able to make free decisions that we are accountable for what we do, and do not do.

Perhaps there is a middle ground here that says that we are not accountable in some respects, but in others we are. In the normal course of events we are reckoned responsible for our moral behaviour, though there may be circumstances in which we are not responsible. Very few of us know how we would react if taken hostage and tortured. No doubt we would all like to think we would behave with dignity, but it may be that deep down we are cowards and our pain tolerance is very low. How far can we be held responsible for cracking under the strain? There will be limits to what we can take. In the normal run of life we accept responsibility for what we do, but in that kind of situation we may be unable to cope because of the person we are. Then we hope that those who hear what is happening to us will understand and accept that we are not responsible for our actions when we face extreme pain. For the most part, then, we accept that we are accountable for what we do, but in extreme cases we allow that people cannot be blamed for what they do, and as we saw in Chapter 7, justice requires that that is recognised.

This is not only true of us in particular situations. Some of us are clearly not responsible for what we do in general. We accept that some of us are simply unable to take responsibility for our lives. This may be so if we have certain medical conditions. It may also be so where someone has a limited idea of the difference between right and wrong.

Such cases are recognised in our legal system. A person who is accused of a particularly nasty crime may have a barrister who, when the case comes to trial, pleads 'diminished responsibility'. That is to say, the barrister claims that the client, perhaps because of the pressure the latter has been under, or because of their personality, was unable to control their actions. In most cases, though, there is no such plea and the accused wants to be treated as though being responsible for what they did. If they are found guilty they are sentenced and this is the way we show our belief that our fellow human beings are accountable for what they do. We do not assume they are robots or that they are sick, but they are responsible for their actions and so must take the consequences. We assume that they have minds and wills and could have chosen to behave in other ways. There may, of course, be extenuating circumstances which a barrister would no doubt explain, but in being brought to trial a client is treated as a person who is responsible for what they did.

Owning our Decisions. As we saw earlier, the nature of moral life is that we all have to take decisions. Mr Jones, whom we met in Chapter 1, is not alone in thinking how wonderful it would be if we could simply know answers to moral dilemmas without having to work at them, but that is not how life is. As we saw, Mr Jones and his friends, and above all Sophie, had to make decisions. Politicians have to decide how much they ought to spend of our limited resources on underdeveloped countries, when our own hospitals need more funds to cut the waiting time of those needing treatment. As individuals it is pertinent to ask if we ought to support local fund-raising to build a hospice when we believe it is the government's responsibility to care for the sick and dying. If we are parents and believe that sex outside marriage is morally wrong, ought we to allow our son and his girlfriend to share a bedroom in our house when they have lived together in their own home for a long time? It is a fact of life that we have to take moral decisions.

An implication of this fact is that having taken a decision we have to own it and live with it. We may wish someone would tell us what to do, but even if someone does, if we accept it the decision becomes ours and we have to live with it. We have to accept responsibility for a decision and own it. It means that when we have decided to act in a certain way we ought not to pass the blame for any bad consequences on to anyone else.

This may have the effect of making us cautious in the decisions we take. Tina and Tom wanted to be married in their local church. In the course of the discussions with the minister it emerged that Tina had been married before, but divorced her husband when he left her. The minister consulted other church leaders about the situation and there was a lot of support for the couple. They feared, however, that if they allowed Tina to be married in church, it would be difficult to say no to others and they were concerned that they could eventually find themselves having to marry people who had been the cause of divorce and who had been divorced more than once, and they felt they could not do that. In effect, they could not live with a decision to marry Tina and Tom in their church because they would have to take responsibility for the possible consequences. Whatever we think of their decision, they recognised their responsibility for what they did and took a safe decision. To the consternation of the other churches in the neighbourhood, while the church down the road says there are limits to what they will do, they work on the basis of taking each case on its merits. It makes life difficult at times because they are repeatedly having to decide, but they are prepared to accept responsibility for what they do.

There is another sense in which we have to take responsibility. In *The Way of Man*, the Jewish philosopher, Martin Buber, wrote about the wise Rabbi Bunam who in his old age said, '"I should not like to change places with our father Abraham! What good would it do God if Abraham was like blind Bunam, and blind Bunam like Abraham? Rather than this happen, I think I shall try to become a little more like myself." The idea was expressed with even greater pregnancy by Rabbi Susya when he said a short while before his death: "In the world to come, I will not be asked, 'Why are you not Moses?' I will be asked, 'Why were you not Susya?'"'

The truth the legend contains is that being human means accepting responsibility for who we are as well as for what we do. Unfortunately, many lives are bound by paternalistic individuals and groups who want to take control of us and shape us to be the kind of person they want us to be to ensure that we live in ways they decree.

We have been looking at the importance of the idea of taking responsibility in Christian ethics. **If ethics means anything at all, it means that we are responsible for what we do**. But more than that, we are also accountable for who we are, and the kind of person we become. It may not be as we would ideally want it to be, but in so far as we are moral agents we must accept responsibility.

What Are We Doing in Making Decisions?

When we were thinking about the distinctive characteristics of Christian ethics in Chapter 9, we noted three things:

- It is based on an invitation to reflect, in some measure, the character of God.

- It involves a relationship with God.

- It is based on a commitment to Jesus Christ.

These three characteristics have a considerable bearing on the way in which Christians understand what happens in coping with the ethical problems of life. We start from our understanding of the character of God, which he invites us to reflect in our own lives. Of the Ten Commandments the first is an injunction to 'have no other God before me'. It puts God at the very heart of Christian morality and hence that must of necessity form the basis of all else that we might want to say about ethics. The biblical implication of this commandment is not simply a call to obey the one who is God because he is Lord, but to be people of love and show his character in our own. This makes Christian ethics an ethic of love, for as we saw earlier, love is God's nature.

Love is such a slippery term. In Western culture it can mean an emotional attraction to someone, even bordering on the sentimental. It can also mean sexual desire. Sometimes, however, we talk of love when there is no sexual element involved at all, but we recognise a friendship in which people have a commitment to each other which results in mutual self-giving and support.

Talk of people loving, then, is varied. In Christian terms one of the features of love is the way in which it issues in action. It is in this sense of love being active on the other person's behalf that it has been suggested that we are not called to like people but to love them, that is, to go beyond our emotional response to them and act for their benefit. When we learned what love is as children, we did it by seeing the way people behaved and being told that was love. We soon learned that it has something to do with being close to each other and showing affection. Perhaps it was a mother asking for a kiss as a sign that the child loves her. Maybe we learned it through the tears and hugs of two people parting, or in discovering something of the intimacy of sex. How else would we learn what love is, than by seeing loving acts?

This is not just a point about how a concept is learned. The nature of love means action for the benefit of others. It can be a painful experience to find that words of love are not confirmed with loving actions. With experience we realise that the opposite is also true: we may meet acts which have the appearance of love, but are counterfeit.

Christians have for a long time appealed to the way in which the Greek language has different words for love. It has a word for a love that is friendship, another for sexual love, another for self-sacrificing, or *agape*, love, and it is this last that is generally thought the most desirable form. This is the love that the apostle John spoke of when he said that God is love. It is also what Paul had in mind when he wrote of love being the highest of the three virtues in 1 Corinthians 13. In Christian ethics it is normally in this sense that love is thought to be so important.

The importance of love is made explicit in Jesus's final words to his followers in the upper room. The record of those last hours is almost a treatise on love: that of God the Father, the love of Christ, and the love of his followers. For our purposes it is the love of the disciples that is of particular interest. Love is the distinguishing characteristic of those who follow Christ, 'If anyone loves me, he will obey my teaching' (John 14:23). It is also a love for other human beings, 'Love each other as I have loved you' (John 15:12). In fact, it is a command from the Lord Christ, 'A new commandment I give you: Love one another. As I have loved you, so you must love one another. By this all men will know that you are my disciples, if you love one another' (John 13:34–5). To call it a commandment is particularly striking because Jesus's approach to ethics was not to lay down commandments. To speak as he did was his way of asserting the importance of what he was saying.

Love matters in the kingdom of God because it characterises those who are responding to the lordship of Jesus, and it is a special kind of love. It stretches to our enemies and that was not always recognised in Jesus's time. To his hearers Jesus said, 'You have heard that it was said, "Love your neighbour and hate your enemy."' Then he added a new dimension. 'But I tell you: Love your enemies and pray for those who persecute you, that you may be sons of your Father in heaven' (Matthew 5:43–5).

A Christian Picture of Decision Making

Thus far, then, we have thought about the way in which Christian ethics reflects the character of God which is love. We have seen that pre-eminently this means a way of life that is based on love:

God

|

Love

Love is not an easy principle to work with, not least because it is open to different interpretations. Although, as we saw earlier, Joseph Fletcher taught that love is the ultimate check on our conventional norms and principles, his ideas do not provide us with clear guidelines as to what we ought to practise. The reason is that love is an abstract idea that needs anchoring in more tangible guidelines, and in thinking about justice we saw one way of doing it.

In practice most of us use concrete ideas to guide us. You may recall that when we thought about Miss Argyle's response to Sophie, one option open to us was to accept that there are principles which exemplify love, and then to use them. This is what most of us do: we set up what are, in effect, sub-principles of love which are more manageable and directive than the abstract idea.

It is hard to know what a definitive list of these sub-principles would be, but some are fairly obvious. Among the rough-and-ready principles that guide us might be the following:

- Always return things that you borrow.

- Do not take what does not belong to you.

- Do not let your friends down.

- Do what you can to help people.

- Do not interfere in other people's business.

- To make a marriage work you have to give and take.

- Live and let live.

- Always tell the truth.

The list could go on. These are the sort of working guides that many of us use in everyday life. Behind them is another list, though, which is a more formal way of expressing our working aids. This would be something like the following:

- Respect other people's property.

- Respect truth.

- Keep promises.

- Respect the right of others to be treated as individuals with dignity.

- Respect the sanctity of life.

- Respect the good name of others.

This too is not an exhaustive list: it cannot be, and it does not have to be.

The significance of both lists is that they express what it means to love:

- Respect other people's property – this is an act of love that protects the share others have of the goods we all need for a full life.

- Respect truth – love implies that others should not be deceived.

- Keep promises – to love others is to respect the plans they may make on the basis of our promises.

- Respect the right of others to be treated as individuals with dignity – love sees them as being of worth.

- Respect the sanctity of life – love is not ultimately destructive.

- Respect the good name of others – our name is our identity. One of the things children do when they want to hurt each other is to make fun of their names. To damage our name is to damage us and that is not a loving thing to do.

These, then, are the kind of principles through which we express our basic principle of love, and can be shown like this:

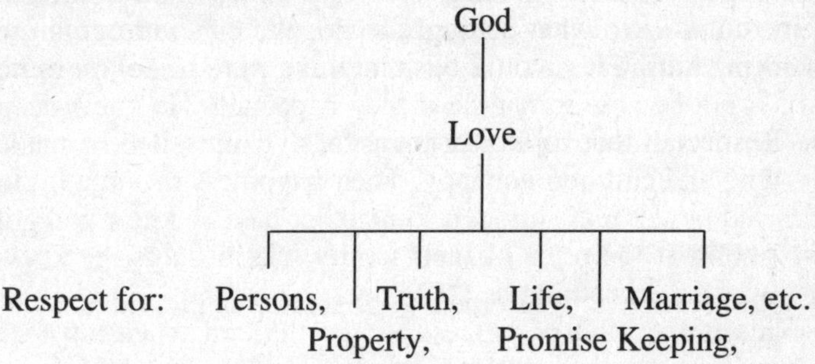

We now have a structure which in part explains what we might be doing in following a Christian view of ethics. But we need to go further, because simply to have principles does not in itself tell us how they ought to be applied, and application is important.

Give a thought to Adrian, for example. He had the opportunity to advance his career, but it would mean moving to another part of the country. How might he set about deciding whether to take the job or not? He might take the advice of someone who has been in a similar position, or he might talk to someone whose advice he values. He might weigh up the impact of a move on those who are close to him. He might think about the way his children's education could be affected and wonder if they would be happy in another part of the country. Is it fair to ask his wife to leave her friends and interests and start again somewhere else? He might recall the problems (and joys) of any previous moves he has made in the interests of his career. Did they make for tensions in the home? Did he find it hard to settle? He might ask how people in his job usually get to the top. He might look at his career models and see what was their path to the top. Then again he might imagine what it would be like to have to start the new job in new surroundings. He might have a sneaking fear that he would not be able to cope at the next level of his career! It so happens that Adrian is a religious man who likes to read his Bible daily. When he realised he might have the chance to move, his reading had a new edge to it as he looked for verses from which he could get some clues as to what he ought to do. We can add one more element: Adrian was conscious that there were some things he would not be able to handle if they happened. He knew deep inside himself that he would never forgive himself if he made his wife and children unhappy. Their happiness meant a lot to him and he felt that although some other men he knew had got promotion at the price of their family relationships, he knew that was not something he could do.

This is the kind of process we go through when we face having to make difficult decisions. It is obvious that Adrian did not identify principles and then apply them. Most of us do not do that either. He searched in a number of directions for guidance, and that is what most of us seem to do. He looked at his Bible to see if it threw any light on the matter. He realised that the people around us may have wise things to say and experience on which to draw. As do most people who are morally aware, he thought about the possible consequences of his actions, both for himself and his family. He became aware of what his conscience was saying to him. Then, too, he investigated how people actually gained promotion in his field. He looked at the example of someone in the job whom he respected.

It is no wonder that when the BBC wanted a name for a discussion programme on moral issues, they chose *The Moral*

Maze. In practice, when most of us pause to reflect, morality is a maze!

We can now add the final layer to our model:

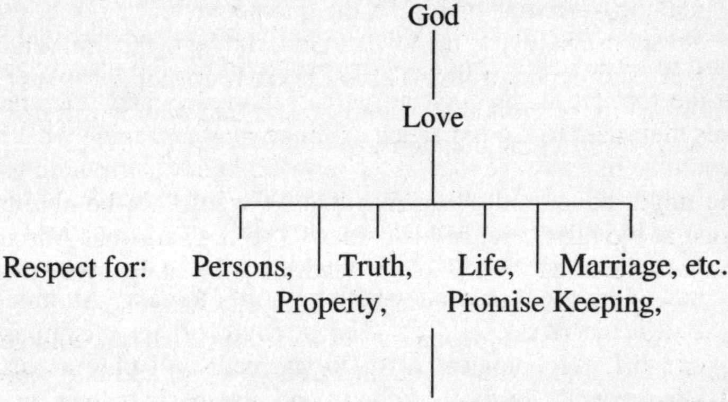

Moral decisions about particular situations using aids such as

- the Bible
- our consciences
- the traditions of our community
- the consequences of our actions
- the facts of the situation

Whatever we believe we ought to do when we face a situation which invites a decision, when we reflect on what happens in practice it becomes clear that we use various aids that help us, though that does not mean that we all use the same aids, nor that we give each the same weight and importance.

The list of aids we may use includes those that are commonly in use whatever our starting point: in Chapter 8 we considered conscience, consequences, traditions, and knowledge. There is also a distinctive tool which Christians use, namely, the Bible. We will think about how that can be used in the next chapter.

Before we think further about decision making, there are two things to bear in mind:

- It is vital to remember that this model is not intended to provide a method by which we can make decisions. It is simply an explanation of the formal structure of our decision making. Christian ethics has the distinctive feature of being a response in love to the love of God, shown in the life, death and resurrection of Jesus Christ. There is no method as such, only a lot of tools that actually come into play in different ways in different situations.

- Behind all of Adrian's considerations, for example, is the kind of person our man is. How does he value those close to him? Are they just there to help him achieve his ambitions and enjoy the increased wealth he hopes to gain? Attitudes will affect what he does. The strength of his intentions, and his psychological drive to succeed, will play a part. His general approach to life, and the basic values that approach implies, will direct his thinking. So too will a host of beliefs he has about people and the priorities of life, not least those he has about God, human beings and the world. It is these that will, in the end, interpret what he hears from his conscience and direct how he will view the likely consequences of what he does, what his tradition says, and what he sees as relevant facts affecting the case.

The Nitty-Gritty

Having a formal explanation of what happens in decision making does not tell us all that may be involved. There are three other features worth noting.

First, **sometimes we have to sort out what the real issue is**. For example, on one occasion the Jewish teachers wanted to trap Jesus into saying something that would give them cause to attack him, so they brought before him a woman taken in adultery (John 8:3–11). What was the issue here? Was it

- the fact of her adultery?

- the question of an appropriate punishment?

- the way in which the teachers were using her?

Jesus's response was to suggest that the first stone should be thrown at her by whoever among them was without sin. In other words he thought the real issue was the way she was being used by the teachers.

The same need to establish the issue is present in the question of intercourse between gay men who are committed to a lasting relationship. Much of the debate about the morality of homosexuality turns on different ideas of what the real issue is.

- Some would say it is about the sex act.

- Some argue that it is about the right of human beings to express their love.

- Some believe the issue is one of acknowledging a person's gender.

What is the issue that is at stake here? There are specific biblical texts that appear to make clear judgments that gay sex is morally wrong. If we check that this is a right use of the texts, then we can accordingly say that the issue is about the sex act, and can then decide what further needs to be done. Homosexual groups, however, claim the issue is more to do with the right to express love. Obviously, the real issue is vital if we are to make correct decisions.

Second, **we need ways of dealing with difficult cases**. As we noted in Chapter 1, sometimes the things we think we ought to do, clash. For example, we cannot always both tell the truth and preserve life. In an ideal world such cases would not arise, but unfortunately moral life is about a complicated and imperfect world. If it were a matter of the simple application of one rule, or one principle to a single situation, it would be relatively easy to translate our ethical ideas into practice. It is usually far more complex than that. There are some well-tried ways of handling such cases. We will consider two of the more obvious.

The first way is to choose what is usually described as **the Lesser of Two Evils,** which says that when we have a decision to make we should choose the lesser of the two evils. If the choice is between telling a lie and someone being killed, then telling a lie is a lesser evil than murder. Both are evils, and whatever choice we make, we will do something that is morally wrong, but in this case one is markedly less so than the other. Usually, Christians who deal with these difficult situations in this way will add that even though we are responsible for doing wrong whichever choice we make, God understands our difficulty and will forgive us.

Thinking in this way may enable us to maintain that lying and murder are morally wrong irrespective of the circumstances. It keeps some objectivity in our ethics, but at the cost of generating a sense of guilt in us. After all, talking about the lesser evil does not remove the fact that it is evil. We cannot say that doing what is evil is of God, for that is just not what God is like. So if we think it right to think about lesser evils, then we have to make a choice and hope we make the right one. The strength of this argument is in the alternative: given we have to make a choice, we would not think of choosing the greater evil.

Circumstances can determine the decision we take when choosing a 'lesser evil'. On one occasion, for instance, we may choose to prevent someone being killed by lying to a homicidal maniac, but in time of war we may think it right to tell where an enemy soldier is hiding so that he can be killed.

This way of handling moral dilemmas does not mean that we always make the right choice, but choosing the lesser evil is a workable way of handling some of life's complexities.

A second way of dealing with difficult cases is to choose **the Highest Principle**. Although this approach is similar to the previous one the assumption here is that there are a number of principles which are more significant than others, and we may not be under the same obligation to do what is right in all circumstances. For example, there may be times when principles such as truth telling and respecting the property of others may need to be laid aside in the light of a higher principle, such as saving life. It is worth noting that in the Jewish tradition any commandment could be broken in order to save life – life being the ultimate gift from God.

This is not simply an arbitrary way of handling difficult situations, but there are grounds for thinking this is a scriptural way of proceeding. When Jesus was asked which is the greatest commandment he replied that it was love for God and our neighbour. He seems to have accepted that there is a greatest commandment (Matthew 22:34–9). Similarly, Paul's description of love in his letter to the Corinthians suggests that there is a hierarchy of virtues, with love at the top (1 Corinthians 13:13).

Respect for other people's property and the negative command not to steal may be principles which on some occasions we may think it right to set aside. Consider the case of someone who has no money and no means of getting any, but has young children to feed. Is stealing a valid way to get food in that situation? The point is that there are cases where we may hold to a principle, but where there are other valid considerations these may cause us to set the first aside in the light of what we take to be a more important principle. In this case it would be the principle of meeting the need for food.

This is in harmony with Jesus's teaching. On one occasion he was taken to task because his disciples took ears of grain to eat on the Sabbath (Mark 2:23–8). The charge was that they were doing 'what is unlawful on the Sabbath.' It was a charge that Jesus rejected because he disagreed with the Pharisaic interpretation of the Law that said that the Sabbath day should be kept holy. To justify his disciples' actions he challenged the authority of the Law when there were other issues involved. He answered the Pharisees, 'Have you never read what David did when he and his companions were hungry and in need? In the days of Abiathar the high priest, he entered the house of God and ate the consecrated bread, which is lawful only for priests to eat. And he also gave some to his companions.' He justified David breaking the Law because there was a need that was more important.

It is interesting to reflect just what the higher principles might be. Does the preservation of life come higher than relieving pain? Or is lying in a good cause higher than Sabbath keeping?

A third feature of decision making is that **we need to face the possibility that our decisions may have both good and bad effects at the same time**. An example is the decision to administer drugs with the intention of reducing pain, even though those same doses of drugs will shorten the patient's life. Here we face a major moral dilemma, for what do we say of the doctors' actions in such cases?

The Principle of Double Effect. There is a **Principle of Double Effect** that is applied in these cases which says that **it would not be morally wrong to produce the effects that we would normally describe as being bad, if we intended the good consequences and not the bad, even though they were foreseen.** In other words, if the bad outcome was a side-effect of the good deed that was intended it would not make the deed morally bad. It is a seemingly strange principle because in such cases we know what the likely outcome is of our actions.

We can state the basis of the principle in four statements:

- There is a difference between directly intending to produce bad effects by what we do, and foreseeing that there will be such effects – in other words, foreseeing the side-effects.

- It is possible to foresee and cause a bad effect without wanting it to happen.

- The bad effect must not come first so that out of that the good effect will arise. This means that this principle does not justify inflicting pain on someone with the intention that in years to come they will be better for it.

- It is legitimate to go ahead with an action that will have bad side-effects as long as there is a genuine intention that a proportionately higher amount of good will result, or that the amount of evil will be reduced.

There is a major weakness in the principle and that is the difficulty of deciding what is intention and what is not desired. This particular weakness has, over the years, led to cynicism about the principle. In the eyes of some critics the principle has been misused, for example, to justify what were effectively abortions among Roman Catholics. If a pregnant woman were to have a hysterectomy, then it would result in the loss of the foetus. It has been alleged that some women were claiming that their intention was to have a hysterectomy and that the loss of the foetus was a side-effect, when the truth was the reverse and the intention was to have an abortion. Given the teaching of the Church against abortion it is understandable that the principle was viewed with a certain amount of scepticism. It did highlight just how hard it is to say what is the intended action and what is the undesired side-effect.

There is general agreement that the principle seems to work better in some cases than in others, and as such is a useful aid as we try to negotiate some of the difficulties we face in deciding what we ought to do.

In this chapter we have used a formal model of decision making – love – which has come from the character of God, on the basis of which principles were selected which underpinned the handling of specific cases. A similar model could be presented by a humanist (see next page):

The two models are alike in their use of principles, but the difference in their starting points highlights the distinctive Christian way of viewing the process of making moral decisions. It is a distinctive way of viewing moral life as a response to the character of God shown in love, for, as we saw in Chapter 9, moral life for Christians comes from a relationship established by God.

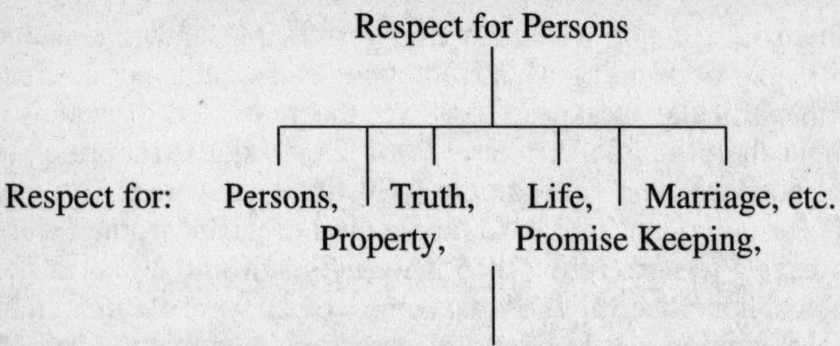

Moral decisions about particular situations using aids such as

- our consciences
- the traditions of our community
- the consequences of our actions
- the facts of the situation

13

The Bible in Christian Ethics

How does a community decide whether it is right for a woman to have an abortion, or for a couple to divorce? How do we unravel the morality of a conflict such as that which has raged in Northern Ireland, where men and women kill to promote what is seen as a legitimate cause? In the Christian community there is a tradition to look to the Bible first for help in finding answers. It is accepted that it is God's Word to mankind, and in the eyes of some the only place to go for direction on what is right and wrong. It is the primary source of moral knowledge for Christians.

While that may be generally accepted, it is not easy to use as a source of knowledge. The Bible is first and foremost the story of God, his world and his people. It is principally a record of the experiences of men and women as they sought to live as God's people. As David Atkinson says in his book *Pastoral Ethics in Practice*, 'The Bible is a story arranged around various themes – of creation, covenant, sin and redemption, pilgrimage, hope and glory – to name a few.' It is the story of people's growing awareness of what it means to be God's family. In telling this story it certainly reveals something of God's thoughts and intentions, but it is primarily a story which is expressed in narrative, laws, wisdom, teaching and poetry. It is not an ethical textbook or manual. It certainly does have things to say about the kind of lives we ought to live, but it is not a series of lists of what counts as good and bad moral behaviour. It is not a rulebook in the same way that a tennis club may issue a book of rules about the conduct expected of members while at the club. Any ethical teaching within the Bible, then, is essentially derived from the story it tells, and that presents a difficulty, for it is hard to understand how a story can function as a set of rules in the way some Christians seem to want. A biography of, say, Winston Churchill, does not set out the law of his time!

The fact that the Bible is not an ethical textbook is important for the way we approach it, and the questions we can legitimately ask of it. It does not say how we are to do ethics: whether we are to look to rules and principles, or to the consequences of what we do, or to any other ethical approach. It is silent on many of the current moral dilemmas we face. It does not have any systematic moral teaching that sets out the moral way for us, and it does not have any explicit account of the values we should adopt. Whatever explicit moral teaching it does contain is scattered. There are bits here and bits there, and even then it is not always clear how they are to be understood. At times actions done in the name of God, or out of loyalty to him, are very difficult to understand.

Nevertheless, the story still has a place in forming our ethics. But if we want to know what the moral values behind the story in the Bible are, we are left to abstract the moral implications of what happened to those people and what their teaching means for the twentieth century. This is particularly true of the Old Testament story. We have to try to make sense of a lot of disparate material which contains many moral prohibitions and laws which the Old Testament writers never put together as a coherent whole.

Yet, despite the lack of precise application, the Bible is still the obvious tool for the Christian community to use in its moral reflection. It makes sense to do so, for as we have seen, Christian ethics is a response to God which is based on his nature, with Jesus at the heart of the life of the Christian community, and Christians believe that the Bible is our primary source in understanding God the Father, his Son and the Holy Spirit.

For centuries it has been, and still is, the Christian's

sourcebook and guide, whether it be in matters of doctrine, liturgy, evangelism or ethics. Though that still leaves Christians to decide how to use it.

The Problem

Apart from the problem of deriving ethics from a story, there are other difficulties in using the Bible as a source of moral knowledge. One is that of interpretation. We do not come to the Bible with open minds, but are the products of our time and read the biblical record in the context of our day. Western Christians tend to bring their Western understanding of words and ideas to the Bible, yet it was written in an Eastern culture. For example, in Malachi 1 we read that God loves Jacob but hates Esau. The word 'love' is understandable, but to say that God 'hates' Esau is not what it seems. It is an Eastern way of saying that Esau was rejected by God as the father of the people of God, not that God has strong feelings against Esau personally.

The Bible was written in the culture of the time, for the people of that time in their immediate context. It was not written for our time and context. If we really want to understand it we have to understand the culture and context from which it came. To understand the significance of Jesus washing his disciples' feet requires a grasp of the culture and, as we have seen, to understand the character of the Ten Commandments we have to recognise the context in which they were given.

There are also difficulties in knowing how we ought to understand the text when we go to it for help in deciding right from wrong. A good example is in the way in which Matthew's account of Jesus talking about divorce contains a clause that says that there are occasions when divorce is admissible. But Matthew is the only Gospel writer to include such a statement. How are we to understand this? Scholars disagree about it, some saying that it is put in by Matthew to soften Jesus's teaching on marriage. Others say it is authentic. Again, there is dispute about the meaning of the Sermon on the Mount. Did

Jesus mean his followers literally to turn the other cheek? Part of the problem is that we sometimes treat the Bible as though it is a series of statements of fact. Yet it includes poetry and metaphor as well as factual statements and we have to decide which literary form is being used in particular passages.

There is another problem: what are we to make of the difficult passages in the Old Testament when God is said to approve and even command the slaughter of whole communities? The problem in understanding these incidents is not misunderstanding the literary style that is being used, but of understanding the character of God, which does not seem to be the same as Jesus Christ.

Then there are the problems that we bring to the Bible. One reason people treat the Bible in different ways is because we find it more helpful to see it one way rather than another. It may be the result of our past and the way we have learnt to see it, or it may be because we fear we will be on the slippery slope of immorality if we do not follow the party line of our particular Christian community and tradition.

Using the Bible

Whatever problems there are in understanding how the Bible ought to be used in ethics are generally resolved, or at least lived with. Christians use it in whatever way they think best fits what they take to be the nature of the Bible. In practice the way that is followed usually comes from the tradition of the Christian group of which a person is part, and often involves what the group understands to be the nature of the authority of the Bible and the extent to which it feels satisfied with the way in which the tradition offers realistic help with contemporary issues.

The result is that there are a number of different ways in which the Bible is used in making moral decisions, and in this chapter we will briefly look at two of them to illustrate different uses. One approach is well established and the other is relatively new.

A Literalist Approach. One approach which has traditionally been adopted by some Christian groups, is that which we met in Chapter 3 when thinking about John Murray. It is a literalist approach in which moral statements are taken at face value irrespective of their context. This means a simple and straightforward morality in which moral standards are decided by appealing to verses that appear to have a bearing on the subject. The result is usually a rule-based ethic where the rules are the absolutes of moral life and the only problem is one of making sure we have noticed all of them. Do not steal, fornicate, tell lies, divorce, and so on, become the focus of moral life.

It is an attractive way in which to use the Bible if only because it gives a sense of certainty about what we ought to do. There are some serious problems with this approach, however.

- It is a generally accepted principle that it is quite unacceptable to take texts out of their wider context. That may be the context of the specific passage or of the wider theological context. We have already seen an example of this being done when we noticed that the Ten Commandments are sometimes taken to be a list of moral prohibitions to be obeyed, while the context actually presents them as a response to God's goodness. In this case an important feature of the Commandments is lost if we do not notice the context.

- It is not just the textual context that is important. It is equally unacceptable to ignore the particular cultural context in which the verse is placed. An example of this is to be found in the fact that when Jesus was discussing divorce in Matthew 19, it took place at a time when there was a serious debate about what were legitimate reasons. His reply needs to be read in that context, rather than seeing it as the definitive word on divorce.

- While people taking this position often ignore the cultural context it is noticeable that they sometimes do invoke it when they want to deny that certain laws apply to them. In his book *Pastoral Ethics in Practice*, David Atkinson makes the point that while Leviticus 18:22 is sometimes used to rule against homosexual intercourse, Leviticus 19:19, which prohibits sowing two kinds of seed, or wearing a coat made of two kinds of material, is ignored, presumably because it is seen as being inapplicable to today.

- Using this approach, how ought we to handle some of the examples of what seems to be presented as good moral practice, but which are questionable by today's standards? For example, in Ezra 9 and 10 there is an account of the return from exile and the realisation that some of the people of Israel had taken wives from the surrounding peoples and had children by them. To take wives from pagan nations was seen as an act of unfaithfulness to God. In his prayer of penitence Ezra talked of it being a disregard of God's commands: it was sinful and evil. The prescribed solution was to send these wives and their children away. This was ethnic cleansing that the international community at the end of the twentieth century would be unlikely to tolerate. Yet, on the face of it, this was acceptable conduct for God's people.

- Those who take this view of Scripture sometimes use particular texts without asking what they mean. For example, they will say that adultery is wrong. If a woman agrees to have sex with an intruder because he threatens to harm her baby is she to be condemned? Is this what adultery means? It is not clear if there is any guilt to be apportioned in this case because there is a problem in knowing if it is a case of adultery. It is a case which invites us to look beyond a simplistic use of proof-texts which say that adultery is morally wrong.

- One of the tests of an adequate ethical position is the way in which it deals with difficult cases where complex issues are involved. Those who take a literalist position will often do what is right in such cases irrespective of the consequences.

An example is that of Thomas More who in the sixteenth century was Lord Chancellor of England. In the turmoil caused by Henry VIII's divorce he was required to take an oath which would deny the pope's authority and assume that Henry's divorce was valid. More knew that if he failed to take the oath he was likely to be put in prison and have his property confiscated. The moral dilemma was very real because that would affect his family's future. Ought he to do what he believed was right and refuse to swear the oath, or ought he to protect the future of his family? Both were morally good things to do, but he could only do one of them. His wife is reported to have said, 'Take the silly little oath, so that you can go free and fulfil your obligation to us.' More refused to take the oath and was punished as expected, and his family suffered. He chose to do what those holding this view of the Bible would see as his moral duty. The obviously wrong act had priority in his thinking, even though it left a duty unfulfilled. We may appreciate the dilemma More faced while wondering if he took the right decision. We can ask if duty overrides other considerations.

We need to be very careful when we try to abstract do's and don'ts and treat them as timeless truths, which is what is commonly done when people appeal to a literalist view of the Bible.

The Bible as a Five-Act Play. A helpful account of the Bible was given by Tom Wright in the Laing Lecture for 1989 in which he discussed what it might mean to talk about the authority of the Bible. He claimed that the real authority for the Christian is not the Bible at all, but the wise creator and redeeming God himself as he seeks to judge and remake the world. He exercises his authority through human beings, so although Jesus claimed that he had all authority he also told his disciples to go and get on with the job of being his people in the world. In Christ there was a new start in the way God's purposes were known, and by the Holy Spirit men were enabled to write the new documents that set out the direction and identity of that new way, the documents we call the New Testament.

It is at this point that Wright offers us a different way of thinking about the role of Scripture. He starts with a recognition that Scripture is mainly a story. How might that help us? It could be by offering us models to imitate, or it could be simply a means of generating an ethos: a general feel and direction as to what life ought to be about. These are rather vague ideas, though.

He asks us to imagine that there exists a Shakespeare play, but the fifth act has been lost. The first four acts provide a great deal of characterisation and the broad direction of the plot can be traced with some certainty. Suppose it was decided to produce that play, but it was thought inappropriate to write a fifth act that would be final and, as it were, make Shakespeare appear to be responsible for it. Suppose further that it was decided to get a group of actors who would immerse themselves in the first four acts and do all they could to understand the forces upon Shakespeare and the way in which he thought. They would then be asked to work out the final act for themselves. They would have to take the play on, while being true to the first four acts. As the final act unfolded it would throw up new situations for the actors, but they would be expected to act in a way that was consistent with the first four acts and within their characters.

Wright goes further. He suggests that we can see the first four acts as representing Creation, Fall, Israel, and Jesus. We even have the first scene of the final act in the rest of the New Testament. But we who have lived since New Testament times have to work out the remainder of God's play, being faithful to what has gone before, and that includes our morality.

If we accept this as a valid way of looking at the Bible, there is an important implication for the way we view the ethical pronouncements in the Old Testament: they do not have the authority in the Christian dispensation which they had in Old Testament days. What was present in the Old has been given new meaning in the New. This fits Jesus's statements, 'Do not think that I have came to abolish the Law or the Prophets; I have not come to abolish them but to fulfil them.' 'You have heard that it was said to the people long ago, "Do not murder, and anyone who murders will be subject to judgment." But I tell you that anyone who is angry with his brother will be subject to judgment' (Matthew 5:17, 21–2).

It means that the Old Testament teachings need to be seen in the context of the New Testament. When Jesus was asked what is the greatest commandment in the Law, his answer was, 'Love the Lord your God with all your heart and with all your soul and with all your mind. This is the first and greatest commandment. And the second is like it: Love your neighbour as yourself. All the Law and the Prophets hang on these two commandments' (Matthew 22:37–40). The command to love the Lord your God was not new. It is in Deuteronomy 6. Jesus used it, however, not as another commandment, but as the all-embracing maxim that summed up all the commandments. It was a new emphasis for a new covenant.

This helps us to put the moral rules of the Old Testament into perspective. They are not to be seen as being invalid, but they need to be reclaimed and they need to be seen as having a new context and a new meaning. They are expressions of the command to love.

Living in the Fifth Act. In November 1997 a High Court in London was asked to order a school to admit a girl, as the child's parents had chosen that school. It was argued that it is a matter of principle that a State school with vacancies should not be able to exclude a child, as this school had done, especially when it was agreed that the girl had good school reports. The school argued that the girl had been refused a place because her father had assaulted the head teacher and another teacher when an elder daughter had been at the school. The ruling was that the head teacher was within the law to act as he did. In the normal course of events we would expect parental choice to be honoured where there were vacancies, but this is a good example of a case where a legal right of parental choice did not apply.

The idea that there may be cases where a principle does not apply has a parallel in the way Tom Wright's view of Scripture may help us. Using divorce as an illustration we can say that in the first act of the play the principle of lifelong marriage was established. Further in the play we meet scenes in which the principle still applies, but not in every case. Initially Moses allowed for divorce in certain cases. Later in the story Jesus restated the basic principle of lifelong marriage but allowed that there might be cases of sexual impropriety when it does not apply (Matthew 19). Then, as the story moves on, we come to the apostle Paul who sees another situation to which the principle does not apply. This time it is that of a non-believer separating from a believing partner.

In some sections of the Church it is traditional to say that there are only two justifiable reasons for divorce: sexual impropriety and a non-believer's desertion. It is perhaps more accurate to say that Moses recognised a situation where the principle of marriage for life did not apply. Later, Jesus too recognised such a situation. Then Paul recognised another.

The story unfolds further as we enter the final act, while being faithful to the previous acts. We find other situations where many would want to say that the principle of lifelong marriage does not apply. For example, in situations where a woman is continually beaten and abused by her husband it would be immoral to require her to stay married to such a man. As the story continues it is likely that there will be other cases where it does not apply, of which at present we have not even dreamt. The point is that at each stage of the development of the story we find there are situations to which the principle does not apply, but this does not diminish the initial intention that marriage be for life.

There is another consequence of accepting this model. In addition to there being cases to which we believe a moral principle does not apply we also find there are applications that are wider than might at first be thought. This is what the disciples found when Jesus extended the meaning of the command not to murder. He saw that the external obedience of rules was inadequate and spoke of its significance for the inner life, so that 'do not murder' is also a charge not to hate enemies. It is not that he made a new rule but that he recognised the fuller significance of the old.

Tom Wright's model is not an arbitrary account designed to make life easier for people who have problems in applying Scripture to life. His model gives an explanation that is true to Scripture itself, but, more than that, it also has affinities with the realities of life. It is for these reasons that it enables Christians to appreciate the circumstances that often surround moral decisions. It enables them to remain true to the moral laws that are the appropriate responses to God's love, yet not be tied to the idea of timeless truths that must be taken literally.

The existence of different models of Scripture suggests that it is a matter of preference which one we choose. However, we have a responsibility to look at them critically and to ask which one gives the best sense of the story of Scripture, for they all purport to be ways of describing the biblical content.

For Christians the Bible is a special source of moral knowledge, but it needs careful use. To say that it is the authoritative revelation of God in his dealings with human beings can be taken to mean that it only has to be consulted for moral issues to become clear. It is not as simple as that and to use it in that way presents a number of problems. As a moral guide the Bible needs to be handled with care and with an openness to the ways in which it unfolds new responses to the God who is love.

Conclusion

The officers of The League of Family Values were divided in their attitude to Sophie's conduct and reflected different approaches to the whole question of human behaviour. They are typical of society at large, where different backgrounds, experiences and beliefs all contribute to different views of morality. When something happens that catches the public imagination as being particularly horrific, like the murder of young children, there is a common recognition that something evil has been done. For the most part, though, people differ in their attitude to the way men and women behave and also to the way in which they decide what is right and wrong.

It might be expected that those who share a common set of religious beliefs would also share common ways of making moral judgments, and in some religions that may be the case. As we saw when thinking about the views of Joseph Fletcher and John Murray, however, this is not the case among Christians. These two thinkers represent totally different approaches. Murray's book was conservative in approach, arguing for an ethic based on obeying rules, while the way Fletcher appealed to the consequences of our actions was very radical. Differences such as these raise the question of why this should be so, and that is what we have been thinking about in this book.

There are psychological factors that influence our ethics. You may recall Mrs Thompson was presented as a lady whose expectation that her needs ought to be met led her to believe that any assessment of moral behaviour had to be seen in terms of her own self-interest. Psychological forces influence Christians. We have seen how a need for security can affect the kind of ethics we are able to handle, so that while some people find a set of rules comforting, others find them constricting, and are therefore less inclined to accept a rule-governed approach. It is also true that being victims of sin can have an impact on human relationships and affect the kind of decisions we take and the ethical position we find most acceptable.

Different approaches to moral decision making is not simply explained by psychological differences, though. Different Christian traditions also influence our approaches. Traditions are important to us, and nowhere more so than in the Church. Different Christian communities have different emphases on moral decision making and on what the important issues are. For example, some believe that the important question is to decide what is right and wrong and then follow a course of action. Others find that too simplistic and want to give a higher place to the effects that actions have on individuals and communities. Some give more importance to their tradition, while others emphasise the role of the Bible, and even then there are different views on how it ought to be used to guide everyday living.

Different views of ethics, however, result from more than tradition. Another reason for the variations among Christians is their different theological emphases. They may subscribe to general Christian doctrines about the Trinity and sin and salvation, but sometimes they differ on the basic question of the dominant idea of God. Is he pre-eminently to be seen as a judge? Or is the most significant way of seeing him that of love? The answer to questions about who God is probably influences the way Christians view moral life more than any other. It affects the way we see human beings and the way we relate to one another and to the world in which we live, and in turn that affects the way in which we respond to moral issues.

Ethics is complicated. In many respects Christians use the same means of making their decisions as non-Christians. We use our conscience and rely on the traditional teaching of our particular group, yet Christian ethics does have distinct features. Christians come from different places and have different goals. We seek to be people who reflect Christ, not just in what we do, but in the kind of people we are. Love is to be our defining characteristic. It is love that is our goal, our motivation and the measure of what we do. The need to love may be understood in different ways, and it may be expressed in different ways, but at the heart of its ethics the Christian Church has the responsibility to work out what loving means. There are no easy answers in making moral decisions, but there is a constant need to keep making such decisions in good faith, using all the aids that are at our disposal, whether they be shared with the rest of humanity, or are unique to the Christian community.

Glossary of Terms

Antinomianism   The view that moral law is no longer binding on Christians, who are under grace rather than law.

Deontological Theories   Deontology is the study of moral duty. It is usually associated with the view that moral judgments are to be made about actions themselves, and not their good or bad consequences.

Double Effect, Principle of   The principle holds that in cases when an action will produce both a good and a bad effect we should intend the good rather than the bad.

Egoism, Ethical   The belief that an action is morally right if it promotes one's own happiness and success, and the consequences are in one's self-interest.

Ethics   The field of study which seeks to explain and justify how we ought to behave.

Existentialist Ethics   The ethics of a school of thought which rejects living by laws, and promotes freedom to be authentic human beings who act in good faith.

Intuitionism, Ethical   A direct awareness of what is morally right and wrong, so that the morality of certain actions is self-evident.

Morality   The ways in which we conduct our lives and behave in relation to what is good or bad.

Natural Law   The moral obligations which can be found apart from revelation, by examining human nature, and by reason. These obligations are applicable to all human beings and societies.

Teleological Theories   Teleologists claim that it is the good that results from an action that makes it a good action, but resulting bad makes it a bad action.

Universalisability   Kant held the view that when we make moral judgments about an action we need to ask if we can consistently will that it will be applicable to everyone facing a similar situation. It means that what is right for me in a given situation is also right for everyone else in a similar situation.

Utilitarianism   Those who promote this position seek the greatest good for the greatest number, where the greatest good is pleasure or happiness.

Utilitarianism, Act   This view evaluates each individual act in the light of its consequences.

Utilitarianism, Rule   This view evaluates the consequences which are produced by following moral rules.